Good Men Great Thoughts:

A Daily Devotional

Authored by

The Brothers of SAM Group

WHPHPH Publishing

The Story of SAM Group

"Looking for a few good men". That was the title of the brief notice in the monthly newsletter of Christ Presbyterian Church (CPC) of Edina, MN that caught their attention. Was it an ad for the US Marine Corps?

Not exactly. It was for a new men's small group, that would meet Saturday mornings at 8 AM, facilitated by two CPC members, Larry Carlson and Frank Pleticha. *"Come check us out. All men invited."* It was an intriguing offer.

What was missing in the notice was the purpose of the group. Was it a bible study group or a prayer group? It didn't say. Was it a service or volunteer group? Or a therapy or support group? What exactly was the group's purpose?

Here's what they learned. Most of the men in attendance were in their 40s to mid-60s. Most had children and several had grandchildren. Nearly half of the men had been divorced. And some had previous experience in men's small groups. For work, they had the self-employed, teachers, entrepreneurs, salesmen, corporate managers, engineers, a limo driver, techies, executives, a few retirees, a financial advisor - even a Fortune 200 CEO. Some were members of the church while others were not. All claimed to be Christian, yet the men were across the spectrum on their faith journey. None claimed to be perfect. Almost all acknowledged the lonely journey men walk. A few said outright they were broken men.

When Larry and Frank were asked what kind of group this was, Frank replied, "A men's group." When asked more directly if it was a Bible study or a service group, Larry responded, *"That's up to us to figure out."*

Most of the thirty or so men who were at the first meeting didn't return for the second - or third.

Yet some kept coming back. A group of ten. Why?

Every Christian man wants to live a good life. To avoid temptation. To close the gap on sin. To avoid the grasp of the Enemy. To be a good man, good husband, good father, good friend, good co-worker and good leader.

But good is often not good enough. What do you see in most Christian men when you walk into a church? Boredom, comfort and indifference.

Someone shared that Thoreau wrote, "The mass of men lead lives of quiet desperation." He asked, *"Did that describe us? Men of quiet desperation?*

A few of the men opened up about their experiences in other men's groups. One volunteered his recent encounter with a traditional Bible study group. After six months, he said he learned quite a lot about the Bible, but he knew next to nothing of the men who attended the course, and that left him wanting.

Another made an encouraging comment, sharing the first thing Jesus did when he started His ministry was to form a small group.

Yet another shared a quote from author and former CEO Bill George who wrote, "We need a small group of people with whom we can have in-depth discussions and share intimately about the most important things in our lives – our happiness and sadness, our hopes and fears, our beliefs and convictions. Not having a small group leaves you alone in the wilderness. They can stretch you, and keep you growing, focused, and connected. Small groups are a must for reinvention."

There was a collective spiritual longing for being part of a group. They had a thirst for being part of something bigger than themselves. The men wanted a group, but agreed they wanted more than just being dutiful, weary Christian men who were good, comfortable, avoided temptation, yet were separated from their hearts.

They agreed they didn't want a typical Bible study class. They wanted camaraderie and to grow individually and collectively. The name SAM was chosen because the meetings were held on Saturday mornings. They created clarity by agreeing on what they did and didn't want as a group. The following are the guiding principles they created:

- They agreed to keep Jesus Christ at the center.
- They agreed they didn't want or need a leader. They would be self-directed. They needed leadership, from all members, but not a leader.
- They agreed to meeting weekly, year-round, every Saturday morning.
- They sought to get to know one another well and to develop genuine friendships with one another.
- In order to ensure transparency and openness, they needed to be able to speak about matters on heart and head with confidence their disclosures would go no further than the room. They agreed to 100% confidentiality.
- They agreed to make no judgements about other brothers. They worked to create a place where they could speak freely about life and their trials and tribulations. Where they could ask questions and brainstorm.
- They agreed to encourage one another.
- They agreed to hold each other accountable to commitments made.
- They agreed to volunteer and engage in service projects quarterly.
- They agreed to take retreats periodically where they could get to know each other better and engage in fun, adventure and fellowship.

- They agreed to commit to growing in their faith, reading and studying books by Christian authors, reading the Bible and engaging in other initiatives that would stretch them.
- They agreed to close each session in prayer and with a reading from a Christian devotional.

And they began meeting every Saturday. They checked in each week to discuss the highs and lows of the week. They celebrated birthdays, promotions, new clients, graduations, accomplishments of their children and family and other wins.

They studied two or three Christian books each year and discussed them. They learned and grew as men together.

They volunteered and served together.

As time progressed, they became increasingly comfortable showing their vulnerabilities and discussing their sins. Yes, they quickly learned that SAM is a safe place. They shared their worries. Worries about jobs. Challenges with children and family members. All the ups and downs. They encouraged each other. They helped each other. Life has a way of beating people down. And everyone needs a cheering section. And the brothers of SAM were there to cheer each brother on. They experienced life together.

They slowed down to reflect on the important questions about life. They've helped one another address and answer questions about what makes them come alive. What stirs their hearts? What are they fiercely devoted to? How can they live more adventurously? Grow spiritually? Become better husbands and dads? How can they flourish and not languish? How can they live in an authentic and masculine way?

They learned the art of storytelling and they dug for, wrote and shared their "Who am I" stories.

They defined their life purposes, clarified their passions and created their unique gift statements and shared with one another and others, too.

They shared with one another, in a round of praise, the qualities they most admired about each brother.

They went on retreats. They take an annual long winter weekend trip - SAM North - to the north shore of Minnesota where they rent cabins, prepare and share meals and hike, ski and snowmobile.

They took a cycling trip to Madeline Island in the Apostle Islands in Lake Superior. And every summer, they pile into one of their brother's lake home in Nisswa, where they fish, waterski, cruise on the pontoon, grill, relax and talk late into the evening around the fire pit.

Most importantly, their friendship grew. They enjoy their time with one another and made SAM group a priority in their lives. They go to ball games, movies and dinners together on occasion.

One of the brothers described SAM group as his "2:00 AM friends." He explained, "I'd feel comfortable calling any one of you at 2:00 AM if I had a problem and needed help. I don't have anyone else in my life who I'd be comfortable calling at that hour."

Another brother volunteered he was closer to his SAM brothers - being able to discuss any matter on his heart or head - than he was to his biological brother. Several SAM brothers concurred.

And yet another said SAM Group to him was the perfect embodiment of Proverbs 17:17, "A friend loves you all the time, but a brother was born to help in times of trouble."

In time, they clarified a description of their unique group that reads:

"We're the SAM Group. A small group of Christian men who meet each Saturday from 8 AM at 9:30 AM at Christ Presbyterian Church in Edina.

We follow Jesus, lift up and encourage one another and live adventurously. While we're not a classic Bible study group - we read and discuss books from contemporary Christian authors as well as read from the Bible. We engage in community service projects. And we take weekend retreats for friendship and fun. We're informal and don't take ourselves too seriously. We work hard, play hard and pray hard. A group of regular guys, ages 40-70, we enjoy life's adventures as we seek to become better men."

Over the years, they've lost one member to death, others to relocation and a few others have just moved on. And they've been blessed to gain new brothers who have heard about and seen the uniqueness of the SAM group and sought to become part of it. Their core group has continued meeting, stronger than ever.

They've given their time, talent and treasure on over twenty occasions to non-profit organizations, most notably their quarterly half-day working sessions with Mobility Worldwide.

They believe in the power of small groups. To a man, they would say their SAM Group has positively transformed their lives. They believe what they get from SAM Group is something they don't get anywhere else. They don't pretend their lives are perfect, but they are each deeply committed to becoming better men, better husbands, better fathers, better friends and to live the lives God intends for them to live.

This year commemorates the 10th anniversary of SAM Group and they have chosen to collectively write *Good Men Great Thoughts*, which contains the quotes, verses and phrases they find most inspiring. By thinking great thoughts, God can transform your thinking and mind.

John Ortberg, acclaimed Christian author and senior pastor of Menlo Church wrote, "What makes people the way they are is the way they think. Think great thoughts! People who live great lives, think great thoughts! Spiritual growth starts with paying attention to our minds. What kinds of thoughts the Spirit flows in."

Do your thoughts lead you to God's best version of you, or away from it? We pray for you that your thoughts lead you to God's best version of you. This daily devotional book is our gift to lift you up and encourage you each day of the year. It's our desire these great thoughts give you hope, faith and inspiration. Thank you for allowing us to share these great thoughts with you.

And – man or woman -- we pray that the Holy Spirit will guide you to a SAM-type of group or inspire you to create your own.

May God richly bless you.

The Brothers of SAM Group:
Chris Bentley, Chuck Bolton, Kurt Hansen, Dave Hemink, Brad Kranendonk, Chuck Leininger, John Meeker, Frank Pleticha, Dave Priddy, Steve Shane, Pat Siebenaler,

Alum Brothers:
Craig Bunker, Will Clarke, Tyler Collins, Curt Cullison, Pete Deutsch, James Emmet, Bill Fruen, Scott Plum, Jim Sargent, Tony Satterthwaite, John Steger

In Memoriam Brother:
Larry Carlson

The Brothers of SAM Group

Chris Bentley relocated to the Twin Cities after his naval career and a divorce that left him searching for meaning and purpose. He gave up corporate life to become a financial advisor. He married Susie, the love of his life, and together they have seven children and six grandchildren. Chris loves skiing, sailing, boating, and cycling, and has brought his sense of adventure to SAM since 2011. God opened a door for Chris when he saw the financial turmoil that many widows experience following the loss of a spouse. In 2017, he founded the nonprofit, Wings for Widows, which helps new widows successfully navigate widowhood. This is Chris' "God-sized dream" and his calling has deepened Chris' faith and his relationships with so many others. Chris' purpose: "I humbly yet enthusiastically guide others down the river of life, helping them navigate the unknown, treacherous waters and financial potholes, leading them to safety to realize their hopes and dreams." Chris' brothers admire his huge heart, passion and enthusiasm for everything he does.

Chuck Bolton is an executive coach and author. He's a founding brother of SAM Group since 2010. With his beautiful and talented wife Mary, they lead their "Fabulous Fourteen" of five children, two sons-in-law and five grandchildren. When he's not working, Chuck loves hanging out with the Fab 14 at the pool or house. He also enjoys cycling, skiing, boating, writing books on reinvention, watching Mary perform live music and attending Twins and Wild games. Chuck's purpose is to guide others through the moguls - so they can see what's possible - and become unstoppable. His unique gift is seeing someone's greatness and understanding their situation, so we can brainstorm possibilities and they can act with inspiration, confidence and commitment. His SAM brothers believe that Chuck's generosity, care for others and energy and enthusiasm are his greatest qualities.

Kurt Hansen, a native of Iowa, moved to the Twin Cities in 1985 with his wife of thirty-seven years, Robin Rubenbauer Hansen. He has spent the past thirty-two years in commercial financing of numerous assets, ranging from rail cars to airplanes. He has four adult children: Lukas, Kelsey, Kathleen and Logan. He enjoys traveling with Robin and his family, spending time at the lake with family, SAM brothers and friends, boating, cycling and snow skiing. He was one of the early members of SAM and enjoys the diversity of each member. Kurt's purpose is to use his energy and God's gifts to make this world a little better than it was the day before. His SAM brothers feel he is honest, generous and always willing to help others out.

Dave Hemink has worked in the medical device sector for over twenty-five years, helping to develop life-changing technologies for patients around the world. He feels very blessed to have found a career that has touched so many, especially those in need. He has been a part of SAM since 2017 and has been deeply impacted by the SAM brotherhood. He is the father to two teenage girls and has been married to his amazing wife for nearly twenty years. They live in Minnetonka and love boating, snowmobiling, hunting and enjoy the many gifts that MN provides. Dave's purpose in life is to break barriers, create paths and to help enable people to live purposeful lives, that positively impact others. The SAM brothers shared that his greatest gifts are the ability to be transparent and to use genuineness to help others.

Brad Kranendonk is a radiologist practicing in the Twin Cities for over twenty years. He joined SAM in 2017 and it has been an incredibly impactful part of his life. He has been active at Christ Presbyterian Church, serving as a deacon and lay care minister as well as singing in the choir. While those activities keep him busy, his real joy in life comes from his family; his wife Michelle and adult children Jacob and Emily. His gift is being a compassionate listener and servant who loves to help others feel better physically, mentally, emotionally, and spiritually. His SAM brothers state his most admired qualities are being a great listener, his willingness to help others, and his compassion.

Chuck Leininger is a retired technology entrepreneur who enjoys serving others. He's been part of SAM Group since 2013. He loves being with his family and mentoring kids in his neighborhood and church. Married to JoDee, Chuck has seven adult children, twelve grandchildren and nine great grandchildren. Chuck's purpose is to be the best example of a Christian, someone who knows he's a sinner, but is trying to do the morally correct things living his life, as an example for his family. He says his greatest gift is "having the time and patience given to me to make sure I'm listening and not missing any opportunities to help those around me, family, friends and strangers. Also, remembering I need to lead by example." His SAM brothers believe that Chuck's most admired qualities are his wisdom, humor and patience.

John Meeker continues to pioneer through the changing tides of life. Originally from Texas, John arrived in Minnesota by way of North Carolina, Michigan and New Jersey. He is grateful for four adult children. He and his wife Kitty have fun with 5 grandchildren...all boys in age from high school to 1st grade. His spiritual orientation is ecumenical and he is especially grateful for a practice developed among SAM brothers: daily journaling. His purposes are fulfilled when others can say that they have stopped circling to scan far away horizons and now have landed to explore and rediscover their own identities. From SAM's readings of C. S. Lewis and through our own experiences among SAM brothers, John reflects on our friendships like this: "The typical expression of opening Friendship would be something like, "What? You too? I thought I was the only one...But once commonality is uncovered, the friend is revealed as a fellow-traveler, one who walks in the same direction."

Frank Pleticha was there at SAM's launch in 2010. As the first meeting opened, Frank was wondering who the Holy Spirit had assembled and how the guys would be used. Little did Frank know that a miracle was in the works. With a forty-year career in marketing research, Frank has learned the power of asking questions and actively listening to the answers. Married to Suzie, the love of his life, Frank has six children and stepchildren, two of whom are in Heaven. Five grandkids joyfully round out Frank and Suzie's life. Frank's true passion is captured by his purpose statement: "I am a broken person who is privileged to introduce other broken people to the Divine Healer, Jesus Christ. I do this through my gift of encouragement, rooted in empathy." Frank's SAM brothers identified these traits in him and Frank gives God all the Glory for wiring him in this way.

Dave Priddy is a sales coach and certified trainer. He has been part of SAM since 2017. He is focused first on family with a daughter, son and daughter-in-law and two precious granddaughters living close by. His wife of thirty-seven plus years, Candy, is a treasure who keeps him grounded as they travel through life as partners. Dave's purpose is to provide encouragement and focus to others to discern how they can be the best "me" possible. His SAM brothers believe Dave's most admired qualities are his compassion, optimism and sense of humor.

Steve Shane is a health-tech product development consultant who lives his life leaving anything he works with better than he found it. He works to enable a healthcare shift to preventative and more effective models through development of new products, and believes his purpose to be fixing the broken healthcare system by bringing useful products to market. Steve joined the SAM group two years ago after his family moved to Minnesota from Chicago, and gets so much out of being part of a group that will drop anything to be there helping each other. He lives in Edina with his wonderful wife of five years Suzie, his four-year-old son Charlie, and his 1-year-old daughter Grace.

Pat Siebenaler is working hard to see himself as a child of God, all the time. It is not an easy task but this group of men has helped encourage, teach and support him in his journey. He lives in Bloomington with his wife, Michele, of twenty-two years and has been blessed with two wonderful children, Emily and Erin. He has been in sales, consultancy and management of critical facilities for over twenty years, which he truly loves. As he draws closer to retirement, he has been on a journey to define what that next phase of life will look like. SAM has been a big part of helping to define that. He has discovered his purpose to encourage seekers and followers in faith to help pursue and/or deepen their relationship with Jesus Christ. To use his gift of empathy and connectedness to earn trust and come along side people to encourage and journey with them in growing their relationship with Jesus.

SAM Alum Brothers on Their SAM Group Experience

Will Clark commented, "As a new guy to the Twin Cities community, SAM Group was a safe space for me to share my observations of Minnesota and my experiences from living in ten states and two foreign countries. I benefitted from the weekly discussions and group events. While I'm certain the burgeoning bonds created would undoubtedly have progressed with my SAM brothers, work took me back to the east coast. I am forever grateful for my continued growth, of which SAM was a key part."

Curtis Cullison stated, "When someone is looking for a group to share life with you never know where it will take you and what it would look like. Almost ten years ago I joined a group of men who were looking to do life together. These men had an impact on me that I failed to see at the time but now see very clearly. Relocation took me away this group but over the last seven years I have called upon some of these men to stand with me in prayer as I faced some very difficult situations. This is what true community is all about. HIS plan is perfect as is his timing, it is up to each of us to open to see the blessings in all things."

James Emmet said, "The SAM Group was at the center of my six years in Minnesota. I arrived from the east coast looking for Christian fellowship and a simpler, less stressful life. I came because of the clean and prosperous city and the lakes, fields and forests. I didn't know a soul in town, but I sought connection. I met them within a month of my arrival and knew immediately that I could trust them. We spoke openly about our challenges and hurts, and about purpose and faith. We each took turns leading the group. While I now live in Florida, the relationships built will last the rest of our lives, and beyond."

A Big Thank You to CPC

It is with an enormous debt of gratitude the SAM Brothers thank the pastoral and support staffs of Christ Presbyterian Church.

Small groups are vital to the health of churches. Especially for large churches - like CPC - small groups are critical as they foster discipleship and friendship. You might feel lost in a mega-church, but you won't feel lost in a small group. It is in small groups where individuals feel a sense of a close-knit community and where the theology taught in the pulpit gets fleshed out in conversation and action.

Small groups are where the personal and collective growth occur, and wisely, now retired senior pastor John Crosby favored and promoted small groups. John was unsurpassed in his ability to deliver inspiring and deeply meaningful sermons. Several SAM brothers have said they would not have joined CPC, had it not been for John's genuineness and powerful messages and lessons. Without John, we wouldn't have had those brothers and, consequently, there would have been no SAM Group.

Pastor for discipleship James Madsen provided on-the-ground support and encouragement to SAM Group in the early days, while Deb Carlson continues to provide resources and ideas to all CPC small groups.

CPC has graciously and flawlessly provided a comfortable room and audio-visual resources so we can meet productively each Saturday. The maintenance team keeps the snow shoveled, the building looking great, and has the coffee brewing early each Saturday morning, never missing a beat, these past ten years. A big thank you to the CPC team for blessing our SAM group.

A Tribute to SAM Group Co-Founder
Larry Carlson
(1943-2015)

As a deacon, tenor in the choir and involved member of Christ Presbyterian Church, the Discipleship Team identified Larry Carlson as a potential leader when they were strategizing their campaign to create more small groups at the church. Small groups, particularly in large churches, are vital for building a sense of community. And Pastor James Madsen knew that Larry, with his friendly and inviting personality, would be the perfect man for the job.

When approached, Larry tentatively agreed, so long as he had a "spiritual wingman" at his side, Frank Pleticha. Frank was a relatively new member of CPC who sought to get involved more deeply in the church. When Larry and Frank were asked to start up a men's group on Saturday mornings, they enthusiastically jumped in.

It's been said that God doesn't call the qualified, he qualifies the called. That was the case with Larry and Frank. Both men took a humble, servant's approach to their new roles. Neither of them had been group leaders before. They actually saw themselves as unqualified for such a role. However, they had faith if they prepared the room and invited the men, the Holy Spirit would provide the rest. And were they ever right!

A tall, strong, yet gentle and humble man, Larry greeted everyone with a warm smile and a firm handshake. After he knew you, he'd put his arm around you, or grab your arm, look at you directly in the eye, and ask *"How are you REALLY doing?"* He genuinely cared, he wanted to hear, he listened, and with Larry, you had all the time you needed to discuss whatever matter was on your heart or head. A rare person who truly cared about others. And the brothers of SAM loved Larry.

Life hadn't been easy for Larry. The only son of a physician who was rarely home, his father pushed Larry relentlessly to excel in school, graduate from medical school and take up the mantle as a family doctor. This proved to be a burden too heavy for Larry to carry, when his mother succumbed to cancer during Larry's senior year of high school.

The grief of his mother's passing overwhelmed Larry. After a difficult experience at the University of Minnesota, and a falling out with his father, Larry moved to Los Angeles to start life anew. As Larry disclosed his story, he lived a colorful life in California in his twenties and thirties. Eventually, he earned both a bachelors and master's degree in counseling and worked as a social worker. Bored by that work, he began driving limousines, and ultimately served as a private driver to Johnny Carson and other celebrities.

In his forties, Larry returned to the church and found great joy in performing in the choir. He was quite talented and performed in venues across the US and Europe. In his early 50s, he reconnected with his high school sweetheart, Mary Jo, and they were married and returned to the Twin Cities, where they joined CPC. At CPC, Larry always looked for ways he could help. He could often be found before or after church services as a greeter, or arranging chairs, or cleaning up after meals or meetings. He said, *"I take joy in doing the little things right."* He always wanted to leave things better than he found them.

Larry loved SAM group. For the first five years of its life, Larry rarely missed a Saturday meeting or a retreat. He insisted he was not the leader and always deferred any recognition or thanks for his role in being a "founding father" of the group. He rejoiced in the successes of his SAM brothers. And when they faced difficulties or struggles, he was always the first to show compassion and empathy. He always had time to talk privately, listen and give sage advice and wisdom when asked. His closing prayers were beautiful. He became a role model for many of the brothers as a man whose life was truly led by Christ. He took great pleasure from SAM group and the impact it had in the lives of the brothers and others who were touched by them.

In early 2014, Larry shared the devastating news with his SAM brothers that he'd been stricken with cancer. He bravely fought his disease before it took his life on April 19, 2015. Upon the news of his passing, one of the SAM brothers wrote in an email, *"Personally, I'm trying to re-frame his final days as his waiting in "the green room" before the big show. In this case, the big show is Larry being ushered into the presence of our Lord, who will pronounce "well done" over his life. Sadness mixed with joy."*

Had it not been for Larry, we would not have had our amazing band of SAM brothers. For that and for many other reasons, we'll remember and be grateful he was in our lives, if only for a short time.

As a tribute to Larry's life, the SAM Group commissioned a new choral anthem, **We Walk by Faith and Not by Sight**, by composer Howard Helvey. The newly-composed piece was performed under the direction of Heather Hood by the CPC choir on November 13, 2016 and can be viewed at Walk by Faith and Not by Sight or **https://tinyurl.com/r3lzm3o.** Larry would have loved the score.

Thank you, Larry, for your love and a life well-lived. Until we meet again.

January

January 1

> "Why, having been endowed with the courageous heart of a lion, do we live as mice?"
>
> *Brendon Burchard, The Motivation Manifesto*

Where in your life are you living like a mouse? What must change as you start the new year? What are you committed to doing differently?

January 2

"When Jesus started His ministry, the very first thing He did was form a small group."

Rick Warren

How would you benefit from being part of a small group? If you are a member of a small group, how can you help inject more energy and life into the group?

> "God grades on the Cross not on the curve."
>
> *Adrian Rogers*

It's never too late. Jesus took your sins on the cross so you can get a fresh beginning, a fresh start. All you have to do is believe in and commit to Him. What changes must you make to honor God going forward from this day?

January 4

> "Don't ask what the world needs, ask what makes you come alive. Because what the world needs are men who have come fully alive."
>
> *John Eldredge*

What are you most passionate about? If you dedicate your energy around your passion and purpose, imagine the impact your life will have.

January 5

> "There is no passion to be found in playing small - settling for a life that is less than the one you are capable of living."
>
> *Nelson Mandela*

Are you playing small ball with your life? What must change?

January 6

> "There's a difference between interest and commitment. When you're interested in doing something, you do it only when it is convenient. When you're committed to something, you accept no excuses; only results."
>
> *Ken Blanchard*

What are you fiercely committed to? What is your cause?

January 7

"Give thanks to the LORD, for he is good; his love endures forever."

1 Chronicles 16:34

What evidence can you see that proves God has and does love you? Hint:
It's everywhere around you!

January 8

> "In the second half of the spiritual life, you are not making choices as much as you are being guided. There are things you cannot do because of who you have become, things you do not need to do because they are just not yours to do, and things you absolutely must do because they are your destiny and deepest desire."
>
> *Thomas Merton*

Are you allowing yourself to be guided by the Holy Spirit? Where are you headed?

January 9

> "Being a dad means raising kids with love, patience, courage, and a firm belief that God is ultimately in charge."
>
> *Unknown*

As a parent, how would you honestly rate the love, patience and courage you show your children and spouse? Where do they fit in your priorities? Would your calendar reflect it?

January 10

> "Do not grieve the Holy Spirit of God, by whom you were sealed for the day of redemption. Let all bitterness and wrath and anger and clamor and slander be put away from you, along with all malice. Be kind to one another, tender-hearted, forgiving each other, just as God in Christ also has forgiven you."
>
> *Ephesians 4:30-32*

Carrying around bitterness and anger is like poisoning yourself and hoping your victimizer will perish. When you forgive, you rediscover the humanity of the person who hurt you. You then surrender your right to get even. Then you revise your feelings toward the person by forgiveness. Forgiveness doesn't mean a reunion. It opens your future for better possibilities - to move past the negative emotions and reclaim your happiness.

January 11

"You can choose courage, or you can choose comfort, but you cannot choose both."

Brene Brown

What areas in your life do you need to show more courage and show less comfort?

January 12

> "Carpenters bend wood; wise men fashion themselves."
>
> *Buddha*

In what areas do you need to grow and reinvent yourself?

January 13

> "I want to learn from the elders that have scars."
>
> *JP Sears*

Who are your coaches and mentors? Who could you learn from that you are not learning from today?

January 14

"A lot of people have gone further than they thought they could because someone else thought they could."

Zig Ziglar

Who could benefit from your encouragement and belief in them?

January 15

"It is not the critic who counts; not the man who points out how the strong man stumbles, or where the doer of deeds could have done them better. The credit belongs to the man in the arena, whose face is marred by dust and sweat and blood; who strives valiantly...who knows the great enthusiasms, the great devotions; who spends himself in a worthy cause; who at the best knows in the end the triumph of high achievement, and who at the worst, if he fails at least fails while daring greatly, so that his place shall never be with those cold and timid souls who have never known neither victory or defeat."

Teddy Roosevelt

Are you the critic? Or the man in the arena? What arenas are waiting for - and needing - you to enter?

January 16

> "I believe in God like I believe in the sun, not because I can see it, but because of it, all things are seen."
>
> *C.S. Lewis*

You do have faith in God, right? Even though you might not be able to see God directly? You don't have to see something directly to know it exists. When you wake up and there's six inches of new snow on the ground, you can be assured it snowed last evening. Look around you for signs of God in your life. What do you see?

January 17

"Set goals so big that unless God helps you, you will be a miserable failure."

Bill Bright

Do you have a God-sized dream? So big that you must have His help to achieve? If not, your dream isn't big enough.

January 18

> "I am thankful for all of those who said NO to me. It's because of them I'm doing it myself."
>
> *Albert Einstein*

Don't listen to ordinary men - they will think your bold God-sized dreams are foolish. Who have you allowed discourage your God-sized dream? What must you do now?

January 19

> "The best way to find yourself is to serve others."
>
> *Mahatma Gandhi*

Who could benefit from your gifts and energy? Who can you help today?
Somebody needs you and is waiting.

January 20

"Injustice anywhere is a threat to justice everywhere. We will have to repent in this generation not merely for the hateful words of bad people, but for the appalling silence of good people."

Martin Luther King, Jr.

Where do you see injustice in the world? What can you - must you - do about it?

"Turning pro is a mindset. If you are struggling with fear, self-sabotage, procrastination, self-doubt, etc., the problem is, you're thinking like an amateur. Amateurs don't show up. Amateurs let adversity defeat them."

Steven Pressfield, Turning Pro: Tap Your Inner Power and Create Your Life's Work

Are you a pro or an amateur? You know the answer. You owe it to yourself and others to step up and show up and operate like like a pro.

January 22

"Tis the most tender part of love, each other to forgive."
John Sheffield

Never go to bed angry. Talk and listen to your partner. Hear what they are saying. Repeat their concerns so they know you understand. Apologize. Say a prayer together. The sun will rise in the morning. Tomorrow is a new day and opportunity to start anew.

January 23

"No act of kindness, no matter how small, is ever wasted."

Aesop

How could you show more kindness today? How about tomorrow? Go show a random act of kindness or two.

January 24

> "No one can make you feel inferior without your permission."
>
> *Eleanor Roosevelt*

Who's opinion carries too much weight in your life? Who makes you feel inferior? What must be done?

> "On a snowy day, he chased a lion down into a pit and killed it."
>
> *2 Samuel 23:20 NLT*

What is your God-sized dream that is so big, it puts you at risk? What's the price you pay by ignoring that dream? What could be the benefit if you committed and chased that dream?

January 26

> "Family is not an important thing, it's everything."
>
> *Michael J Fox*

Do your priorities and calendar reflect that family is your #1 priority?

January 27

> "He who fears he will suffer, already suffers because he fears."
>
> *Michel De Montaigne*

Where are you letting fear hold you down? Do you agree that FEAR is False Evidence Appearing Real?

January 28

> "All that is necessary for the triumph of evil is that good men do nothing."
>
> *Edmund Burke*

There is much evil in the world. What is one cause of evil that you should take action on? Where enough is enough?

January 29

As it says on the wall at Mobility Worldwide, one of our favorite charitable causes, that assembles and distributes hand-propelled carts for people who are leg-disabled in third world countries, "If you have the ability to respond then you have a response-ability".

Mobility Worldwide

What need could use your skills and efforts? What cause can you be response-able toward?

January 30

"All men die, few men ever really live."

William Wallace

What cause have you fiercely committed yourself to?

January 31

> "Tell me and I forget, teach me and I may remember, involve me and I learn."
>
> *Benjamin Franklin*

Could you do more involving, coaching and encouraging, rather than telling and teaching in your life at work and home?

February

February 1

> "Good works do not make a good man, but a good man does good works."
>
> *Martin Luther*

What are the good works that you are doing? OK, fine. Now what are you doing to become a better man? A better follower of Christ? What have you committed to doing to reinvent yourself and grow as a man?

February 2

"We are not an advertisement for Jesus; we're supposed to be
evidence"

Bob Goff

Many Christians act in ways that are antithetical to "What Jesus Would Do."
Forget about your claim that you are a Christian. If someone who didn't
know you observed your actions, or inactions, would that person be able to
claim, "Yes, you are Christ-like in your actions"?

February 3

"God never said that the journey would be easy, but He did say that the arrival would be worthwhile"

Max Lucado

Are you seeking comfort or a journey in your life?

February 4

"An institution is the lengthened shadow of one man."

Ralph Waldo Emerson

You are the leader of your job, home and life. Are you having positive impact on everyone with whom you interact?

February 5

> "Smart people don't fail because they don't know. They fail
> because they don't apply themselves. They lack the commitment
> and determination needed to overcome adversity."
>
> *Scott Plum, author of Taking Off Into the Wind: Creating Lift Out of Life*

How can you become more resilient and overcome adversity?

February 6

"Reflect upon your present blessings, of which every man has plenty; not on your past misfortunes, of which all men have some."
Charles Dickens

Charles Dickens

Starting the morning writing down three things you are grateful for and why you are grateful for these blessings - every day in a journal - is one of the most life-enhancing and rewarding habits you can develop. Add this to your daily routine.

February 7

> "A pessimist sees the difficulty in every opportunity; an optimist sees the opportunity in every difficulty."
>
> *Winston Churchill*

How's your level of optimism? Where could you be more optimistic in your life? Ask God to help make your dreams come true. He's listening...and waiting.

February 8

> "God's power works best in my weakness."
>
> *2 Corinthians 12:9*

What area of your life do you most need God's blessings? Have you asked
in prayer for God's help?

February 9

"My negative feelings don't come from God so I don't have to put up with them!" 2 Timothy 1:7

2 Timothy 1:7

Negative feelings you experience come from your mind, not God. Identify those feelings and let them go. Here's a little story: A pastor in training from the Philippines committed a sin while in seminary. He confessed. The minister he confessed the sin to died. He was still troubled by it. Years later, he met a 10-year-old girl who said she was talking with God. He said "Really? Well, can you ask him to forgive me for the sin I committed while in seminary?" The little girl turned away and prayed for two minutes. She turned around and said, "God said he forgot about it and you should to." We need to ask forgiveness from God before we forgive ourselves. We need help from the outside. What sin or negative circumstance do you need to pray about, let go and forget about?

February 10

"When you are shaken out of your comfortable routines, grip My hand tightly and look for growth opportunities. Instead of bemoaning the loss of your comfort, accept the challenge of something new. I lead you on from glory to glory, making you fit for My kingdom. Say yes to the ways I work in your life. Trust Me, and don't be afraid."

Sarah Young, Jesus Calling

How could more trust in God impact your life and the lives of others? Are you asking God for his direction for your life? Are you trusting God?

February 11

"God changes caterpillars into butterflies, sand into pearls and coal into diamonds using time and pressure. He's working on you too."

Rick Warren

It's hard to see sometimes, but reflect on the last few years. How has God worked on and changed you?

February 12

"Everything you want is on the other side of fear"

Jack Canfield

Take the first step. God will show you the next step and the next step. Will today be the day to take your first step?

February 13

"Blessed are those who have not seen and have yet believed."
John 20:29

Faith is having complete trust or confidence in someone or something - even if you can't see it. What do you have absolute faith in?

February 14

> "So, remember these three things that shall always continue: faith, hope and love. And the greatest of these is love"
>
> *1 Corinthians 13:13*

Would your spouse and family say you show them the love they crave and deserve?

February 15

> "When we lose one blessing, another is often most unexpectedly given in its place."
>
> *C.S. Lewis*

What recent blessings have you experienced?

February 16

> "Most people dread finding out when they come to die that they have never really lived."
>
> *Thoreau*

If you died tomorrow, what would you most regret? What area or person of your life needs your immediate attention and effort? What risks have you not taken that you may regret if you don't? What opportunities are out there you might regret not taking?

February 17

"The best and only safe road to honor, glory, and true dignity is justice."

George Washington

Where do you see unfairness and injustice in your world? What are you doing about it?

February 18

"The secret of success is to find a need and fill it, to find a hurt and heal it, to find somebody with a problem and offer to help solve it."

Robert Schuller

Where do you have an opportunity to serve by helping someone with a problem - now?

February 19

"If we don't listen to everything that the spirit of God has to say, eventually we won't hear anything."

Mark Batterson

You don't get to cherry pick. To get more from God, get into God's word. Read and follow the Bible. Read great books by Christian authors. Hint: There's a list of great books that focus on the spirit of God at the end of this book. Check it out and jump into a book or two.

February 20

> "Where there is no vision, the people perish."
>
> *Proverbs 29:18*

What's your vision for your life? What's your purpose? What's your vision for your marriage and family? These are important questions to answer. Grab your journal, reflect, meditate and write out your visions of a purposeful life.

February 21

> "If today were your last, would you do what you're doing? Or would you LOVE more, GIVE more, FORGIVE more?"
>
> *Max Lucado*

Taking a look at your calendar and priorities, are you spending your time and energy on the people and causes you love most? Where do you need to adjust to match your calendar with your true priorities?

February 22

"Nurture your mind with great thoughts. To believe in the heroic makes heroes."

Benjamin Disraeli

What great thoughts are you taking in daily to lift your spirits and inspiration?

February 23

> "Even if you're on the right track, you'll get run over if you just sit there."
>
> *Will Rogers*

You know what needs to be done. What three actions can you take to move things forward today?

"Those who advance do so because they value action itself. They feel that positive forward momentum - progress - is a reflection of their character, and so they take pride and satisfaction in actions toward that end. They think, "If I am not taking significant action to advance and progress in life, I do not feel as happy, engaged, successful or giving." Psychologically, much is at stake based on their sense of proactivity, growth and advancement in life.

Let us remember that humankind must be measured, by actions alone, not intentions. What we intend is of little importance when judging our character or gauging our happiness. Only action reveals our true selves. Only action moves us to mastery. Only action allows us to create, grow, connect, contribute, rise to our highest selves, and soar into the bright stratosphere of greatness. All else is merely thought, and there is a difference between intention and initiative.

All that we want to feel in life - happiness, joy, satisfaction, peace, success, love - can be felt only because of our actions."

Brendon Burchard, The Motivation Manifesto: 9 Declarations to Claim Your Personal Power

Matthew 7:16 "You will know them by their fruits." Are you taking sufficient action to lead an impactful life? How could you make a greater impact with the gifts you've been given?

February 25

> But the Lord has become my fortress, and my God the rock in whom I take refuge.
>
> *Psalm 94:22*

When your days are dark, do you find God your fortress?

February 26

"Never cry for anything (or anybody) that won't cry for you."

Bob Proctor

What thing or person are you giving entirely too much of your attention to? What will you commit to doing differently after reminding yourself of Bob Proctor's sage advice?

February 27

"You are the only Bible some unbelievers will ever read."

John MacArthur

Every morning, do you ask "What Jesus would do?" as you prepare for the day?

Commit to telling more and better stories. Why?

"Those who tell the stories rule society." - Plato

"Scratch the surface in a typical boardroom and we're all just cavemen with briefcases, hungry for a wise person to tell us stories." - Alan Kay

"The highest-paid person in the first half of this century will be the storyteller. All professionals, including advertisers, teachers, entrepreneurs, politicians, athletes and religious leaders, will be valued for their ability to create stories that will captivate their audiences." - Rolf Jensen

Bottom line, we learn from stories. And we need to hear your stories!

Plato, Alan Kay, Rolf Jensen

Do you use storytelling to capture the hearts and heads of others? Could you use storytelling more effectively in your life?

February 29

"Bless our God, O peoples!

Give him a thunderous welcome!

Didn't he set us on the road to life?

Didn't he keep us out of the ditch?

He trained us first,

passed us like silver through refining fires,

Brought us into hardscrabble country,

pushed us to our very limit,

Road-tested us inside and out,

took us to hell and back;

Finally he brought us

to this well-watered place."

Psalm 66:8-12

Do you agree that believing in and being with God in heaven is worth any worldly discomfort? Why or why not?

March

March 1

> "He who has a Why to live can bear almost any How."
>
> *Nietzsche*

What's the purpose of your life?

March 2

"The ultimate measure of a man is not where he stands in moments of comfort and convenience, but where he stand at times of challenge and controversy."

Dr. Martin Luther King, Jr.

How does staying in your "comfort zone" prevent you from making a bigger impact with your life?

March 3

"A word of encouragement from a teacher to a child can change a life. A word of encouragement from a spouse can save a marriage. A word of encouragement from a leader can inspire a person to reach her potential."

John C Maxwell

Who needs to hear your encouragement today? Can you make a commitment to encourage at least one person each day for the next thirty days? Your 30-day encouragement challenge.

March 4

> "If you want to build a ship, don't drum up people together to collect wood and don't assign them tasks and work, but rather teach them to long for the endless immensity of the sea."
>
> *Antoine De Saint-Exupery*

Are you micromanaging people? Or, inspiring people with a grand vision of the future?

> "What's the purpose of our leadership team? Our purpose is to bring clarity, alignment and intensity. What is it that we want to get done? Are we aligned in order to be able to get it done? And are we pursuing that with intensity? That's really the job."
>
> *Satya Nadella, CEO, Microsoft*

Where do you need to create greater clarity? Who do you need to get better aligned? How can you bring more intensity and inspiration to the cause?

March 6

> "Every man dies. Not every man really lives. When you play the man, when you make the man you are lighting a candle for the next generation - a candle that shall never be put out. Play the man! Make the man!"
>
> *Mark Batterson, author of Play the Man: Becoming The Man God Created You To Be*

Are you playing the man in your life?

March 7

"Nothing ever comes to one, that is worth having, except as a
result of hard work."

Booker T Washington

Are you putting in the right effort to the right causes in your life to create
the impact you are capable of?

March 8

"No one will be remembered for what they just planned to do."

Bob Goff

On a scale of 1-10, how do you rate your production? Your execution? It's always better to have a good plan excellently executed, than an excellent plan executed in a mediocre way.

March 9

"Your purpose will only be found in service to others, and in being connected to something far greater than your body/mind/ego."

Wayne Dyer

Do you have a purpose bigger than you that you serve? If not, how could your life improve by finding one?

March 10

> "You can easily judge the character of a man by how he treats those who can do nothing for him."
>
> *James D. Miles*

Do you treat everyone well? Would everyone agree?

March 11

"If your life is off-key, maybe it's because you've been deafened by the negative self-talk that doesn't let God get a word in edgewise."

Mark Batterson, author of Whisper: How to Hear the Voice of God

Do you take time daily to pray and meditate to hear God's word? Or are you too busy with distractions, addicted to social media and TV and your own circular self-talk?

"I received a book on my birthday from a dear friend: Sailing True North. Ten Admirals and the Voyage of Character. The book was written by Admiral (retired) James Stavridis. He is a 1976 USNA graduate; I was a USNA '79 graduate. He's actually spoken here in the Twin Cities before, and I got to hear him. Now I'm reading his fascinating book, a book about men of character. It's inspiring. I read it and want to be like them. I want to be my best. The man God intended. From a chapter in the book:

Themistocles (one of the ten admirals) says to inspire his men in one of the most lopsided naval battles of all time:

"Men of Athens! Free men of Athens! When you take up your oars today, you take in your hands the destiny of our city, of our families, of our way of life. If today we fail, with us will die the hopes of all, and the hopes of freedom for any. We must not fail - we shall not fail.

Today, this day, we must row as we have never rowed before! For today, men of Athens - we will row for Freedom!"

After persuading his outnumbered troops to "row for freedom," Thermistocles put to sea to face the superior Persian navy.

Despite all odds, it was an extraordinary victory, and one that is still studied at the Naval Academy today. It defined Thermistocles' character as one of the great leaders - admirals - of all time.

I pray to our Lord that he continue to shape my character, to be a leader of others, to fear none, to love all, and to be victorious."

Sailing True North by Admiral (retired) James Stavridis, Themistocles

Are you rowing with intensity with your life, as you would if you were rowing for freedom?

March 13

> "Great minds have purposes, others have wishes."
>
> *Washington Irving*

Is your life driven by a purpose? If not, could it be? If yes, what could be your purpose?

March 14

"To be successful you've got to have a dream, a vision, a burning passion, and a magnificent obsession. This dream, goal, obsession has to become your prime motivator. It takes enthusiasm, commitment, pride, a willingness to work hard, a willingness to go the extra mile, a willingness to do whatever has to be done in order to get the job done."

Jeffrey J. Mayer

What cause is worth committing your passion and motivation to?

March 15

> "The only limit to your impact is your imagination and commitment."
>
> *Tony Robbins*

What would be the vision for your life if you knew you could accomplish anything? What's your commitment to bringing that vision to life?

March 16

Asked how he would like to be remembered, Supreme Court Justice Thurgood Marshall replied, "That he did what he could with what he had."

Thurgood Marshall

Could it be truthfully said at your funeral that "he did what he could with what he had?" If not, what must you start and stop, starting today?

March 17

> "Get involved in something that you care so much about that you want to make it the greatest it can possibly be, not because of what you will get, but just because it can be done."
>
> *Jim Collins*

What must get done that you can do if you throw yourself behind it with 100% commitment?

March 18

"You only have to succeed the last time."

Brian Tracy

Where have you quit prematurely? On what topic or issue can you
continue to chip away at, until success occurs?

"Meaning is not something you stumble across, like the answer to a riddle or the prize in a treasure hunt. Meaning is something you build into your life. You build it out of your own past, out of your affections and loyalties, out of the experience of humankind as it is passed on to you, out of your own talent and understanding, out of the things you believe in, out of the things and people you love, out of the values for which you are willing to sacrifice something. The ingredients are there. You are the only one who can put them together into that unique pattern that will be your life. Let it be a life that has dignity and meaning for you. If it does, then the particular balance of success or failure is of less account."

John Gardner, a politician and a recipient of the 1964 Presidential Medal of Freedom, on how to live a meaningful life.

Have you discovered your meaning or purpose? If not, is that a cause worth undertaking?

March 20

> "People rarely succeed unless they have fun in what they are doing."
>
> *Dale Carnegie*

How can you bring more fun to your work? How can you change your thinking to experience more joy where you labor?

March 21

"Strive not to be a success, but rather to be of value."
Albert Einstein

Where - and to whom - can you be more valuable?

March 22

"Twenty years from now you will be more disappointed by the things that you didn't do than by the ones you did do, so throw off the bowlines, sail away from safe harbor, catch the trade winds in your sails. Explore, Dream, Discover."

Mark Twain

What dreams and ideas have you been too fearful to pursue? Is it time to pursue? It not now, when?

March 23

> "Give me six hours to chop down a tree and I will spend the first four sharpening the axe."
>
> *Abraham Lincoln*

Have you prepared a good plan to pursue the number one goal that is most important to you?

March 24

> "Your first and foremost job as a leader is to take charge of your own energy, and then to help orchestrate the energy of those around you."
>
> *Peter Drucker*

Are you the custodian of your own energy? Your physical, mental, emotional and spiritual energy? Are you both expending and renewing your energy?

March 25

> "As we express our gratitude, we must never forget that the highest appreciation is not to utter words, but to live by them."
>
> *John Fitzgerald Kennedy*

Do you walk your talk? Would others say you do?

March 26

> "Decide whether or not the goal is worth the risks involved. If it is, stop worrying."
>
> *Amelia Earhart*

Do you let worry overwhelm you? Don't! Pray on it and move forward. One step at a time.

March 27

"Busyness is the great enemy of friendships."

Rick Warren

Would your friends say your relationship has suffered due to your busyness? What should you do to reignite and recharge your friendships? What's the next step?

March 28

"Everyone thinks of changing the world, but no one thinks of changing himself."

Leo Tolstoy

Do you believe in the old saying, "You are either getting better or you are getting worse"? In what areas do you need to grow, reinvent and change?

March 29

"You can't go back and change the beginning, but you can start
where you are and change the ending."

C. S. Lewis

Today is a new day. What can you do today to change the story?

March 30

> "I don't know what your destiny will be, but one thing I know: the only ones among you who will be really happy are those who will have sought and found how to serve."
>
> *Albert Schweitzer*

You are here to serve. How can you better and more effectively serve, to create an even greater impact?

March 31

"Let us never forget that government is ourselves and not an alien power over us. The ultimate rulers of our democracy are not a President and senators and congressmen and government officials, but the voters of this country."

Franklin D. Roosevelt

We live in a holistic world. Where and how do you need to better serve all the stakeholders in your life - not just the most powerful?

April

April 1

> "Love makes you kind. And kindness makes you likable. When you're kind, people want to be around you. They see you as being good to them and good for them."
>
> *Unknown*

Love isn't convenient and takes slowing down to be present. Today, slow down to show your kindness and love for those around you. Who needs to feel your kindness and love?

April 2

"Christ the Lord is risen today, sons of men and angels say. Raise your joys and triumphs high; sing, ye heavens and earth reply."

Charles Wesley

Give praise for the day and the blessings each day brings. How can you be a blessing to others today? How are others being a blessing to you? Give thanks.

April 3

> "For the eyes of the Lord search to and fro throughout the earth to strengthen those whose hearts are fully committed to him."
>
> *2 Chronicles 16:9*

If you're fully committed to the Lord today, you're being strengthened in a way that surpasses anything that you could obtain from this world. Embrace that strength that you're being given and run with it.

Are you all in with your relationship with Jesus? Explore that relationship today with Jesus knowing he is looking to strengthen you.

To help prepare our hearts for Holy Week, John Piper writes about Jesus' manhood:

"In his perfect manhood, Jesus was not self-sufficient. He looked to his Father for all that he needed in order to do the Father's will. He knew that he must die. And he knew that without the sustaining power of his Father, the weakness of his human flesh would fail in the hour of trial. So, he prayed."

John Piper

Do you pray in your weakness to find strength in Jesus and the promises of Our Father? Today submit to Jesus your weaknesses and find strength in Him.

"Praise be to the God and Father of our Lord Jesus Christ, the Father of compassion and the God of all comfort, who comforts us in all our troubles, so that we can comfort those in any trouble with the comfort we ourselves receive from God. For just as we share abundantly in the sufferings of Christ, so also our comfort abounds through Christ."

2 Corinthians 1:3-5

Here we find a "So That" statement, He comforts us "So That" we can in turn comfort others. Today rest in this statement, find comfort in Jesus and in turn apply that love extended to you to someone around you.

April 6

> "He has shown you, O man, what is good. And what does the Lord require of you? To act justly and to love mercy and to walk humbly with your God."
>
> *Micah 6:8*

What does it look like to walk humbly with God? On a walk, side by side, guards down, walking with a friend. As believers, we have this relationship with Him.

"Always be prepared to give an answer to everyone who asks you the reason for the hope you have. It is easier to obey this command when you're well rested and your life is flowing smoothly. It's quite another matter when you're feeling exhausted and frazzled. Yet this may be the time when your hopeful answer will make the greatest impact. So make it your goal to be prepared always. You need to be ready to answer everyone who asks you the reason for your hopefulness. It is tempting to judge some people as poor candidates for learning about Me and what I mean to you. But only I know their hearts and the plans I have for them.

Essential preparation for giving a good answer is living in awareness of My Presence - trusting Me fully as your Hope. This will steady you as you deal with the frequent ups and downs of your life. Whenever you're struggling, encourage yourself by pondering truths of the gospel in by gazing at Me, your glorious Hope."

Jesus Always, Sarah Young

In today's world, the definition of Hope points to material or situational improvements. Here Sarah Young points our Hope to something Eternal. Our hope is being with Him eternally and what we are experiencing today is temporary compared to eternity. Have a great day and try to focus on your eternal Hope. Pay attention to how your day goes.

April 8

> "Remember finally, that the ashes that were on your forehead are created from the burnt palms of last Palm Sunday. New beginnings invariably come from old false things that are allowed to die."
>
> *Richard Rohr*

Fields need the mulch of the past planting to replenish the nutrients for future plantings. The imagery here reminds us that death is needed to bring new life. Where do you see this in your life?

If you make the Lord your refuge, if you make the Most High your shelter,

no evil will conquer you; no plague will come near your home.

For he will order his angels to protect you wherever you go.

They will hold you up with their hands so you won't even hurt your foot on a stone.

You will trample upon lions and cobras; you will crush fierce lions ("RUN TO THE ROAR!") and serpents under your feet!

The Lord says, "I will rescue those who love me. I will protect those who trust in my name.

When they call on me, I will answer; I will be with them in trouble. I will rescue and honor them.

I will reward them with a long life and give them my salvation."

Psalm 91, beginning at Verse 9

What do you do to make the Most High your refuge. Think about how to apply this today and in this long life.

April 10

> "They found the stone rolled away from the tomb, but when they entered, they did not find the body of the Lord Jesus."
>
> *Luke 24: 2-3*

Imagine how you would have felt as a follower of Jesus and finding that tomb empty JUST as Jesus said it would be. Would you be living your life differently today?

April 11

> "Forgiveness is for YOU, not the other person. Holding a grudge weighs down your spirit and can make you become a person you don't want to be."
>
> *Joanna C Smith*

Tomorrow is Easter. You will likely be with family and friends. Is there someone you need to release and forgive?

April 12

> "Now, brothers and sisters, I want to remind you of the gospel I preached to you, which you received and on which you have taken your stand. For what I received I passed on to you as of first importance: that Christ died for our sins according to the Scriptures, that he was buried, that he was raised on the third day according to the Scriptures"
>
> *1 Corinthians 15*

Rest in this truth. It is finished. There is salvation in His death, freely given for you. Go in the peace of our Lord and Savior and live the gospel in your life today.

April 13

"Faith is the bridge between where I am, and the place God is taking me."

Unknown

What are you struggling with today that you need to trust in faith that God has control of the situation?

"We can rejoice, too, when we run into problems and trials, for we know that they help us develop endurance. And endurance develops strength of character, and character strengthens our confident hope of salvation. And this hope will not lead to disappointment. For we know how dearly God loves us, because he has given us the Holy Spirit to fill our hearts with his love."

Romans 5:3-5

In our time of trials seems the times we grow in relationship and trust in Jesus. If we turn to Jesus, He fills our hearts with the Holy Spirit and His love. Where in your life do you need to turn to Jesus today?

April 15

> "The glory of God is a man fully alive."
>
> *St. Irenaeus*

When filled with the Holy Spirit, do you see yourself fully alive?

April 16

"Religion says, I Obey: Therefore I am accepted. Christianity says, I'm accepted therefore I obey."

Tim Keller

Focus on your identity in Jesus today, feel that He loves you.

April 17

> "Do all the good you can,
>
> By all the means you can,
>
> In all the ways you can,
>
> In all the places you can,
>
> At all the times you can,
>
> To all the people you can,
>
> As long as ever you can."
>
> *John Wesley*

And how can you do all of this? Is it through Jesus who gives you strength? Turn to Jesus and place this yoke on Him who gives you strength.

April 18

"Lives that have been raised from death by Jesus' sacrifice should be willing to make daily sacrifices to meet the needs of others."

Unknown

Today set aside yourself for a friend, in Jesus' name.

April 19

> "What Good Friday and Easter accomplished for us:
>
> You know that you were ransomed from the futile ways inherited from your ancestors, not with perishable things like silver or gold, but with the precious blood of Christ, like that of a lamb without defect or blemish."
>
> *1 Peter 1:18-19*

Reflect on this past week following Easter, has the precious blood of Christ outshone the perishable silver and gold in your life?

April 20

"There is real wisdom, Lord, in the adage 'It is always Springtime in the heart that loves God.' Springtime is a season of optimism and hope, and the Christian lives a faith centered on hope. Winter, with its cold and dark days has gone, just as Good Friday has passed to Easter and beyond. We live a resurrection life reflected in the new life springing up around us. Thank you, Lord, for the hope that you bring, the renewal that you bring, both to this world and to our hearts and lives."

Christian Prayers for Spirit

What springtime element brings you joy in God's wonder on earth?

> But he said to me, "My grace is sufficient for you, for my power is made perfect in weakness." Therefore I will boast all the more gladly about my weaknesses, so that Christ's power may rest on me. That is why, for Christ's sake, I delight in weaknesses, in insults, in hardships, in persecutions, in difficulties. For when I am weak, then I am strong.
>
> *2 Corinthians 9-10*

Our culture doesn't rejoice in weakness typically but in Christ we are to delight in it for I am strongest when I am weak. What does this concept mean to you and how do you apply it in your life today?

April 22

> "I pray that out of his glorious riches he may strengthen you with power through his Spirit in your inner being, so that Christ may dwell in your hearts through faith.
>
> And I pray that you, being rooted and established in love, may have power, together with all the Lord's holy people, to grasp how wide and long and high and deep is the love of Christ, and to know this love that surpasses knowledge —that you may be filled to the measure of all the fullness of God."
>
> *Ephesians 3:16-19*

Yesterday we focused on our weaknesses making us strong. Here we see Christ filling us with His spirit making us strong through faith in Him. Today search for His spirit to fill you up and experience how wide and long and deep is the love of Christ.

April 23

> "There are no secrets to success. It is the result of preparation,
> hard work and learning from failure."
>
> *Colin Powell*

Think of a time where you fell short of expectations and how you recovered
from it. What did you learn from it and did it draw you closer to God?

April 24

> "Life is 10% what happens to me and 90% how I react to it."
> *Charles Swindoll*

What do your reactions look like? Where are you drawing from in those reactions?

April 25

"Satan lives in our secrets. What we don't confess, he owns."

Abby Johnson

What secrets to you keep in the dark? What happens when you shed light on them?

April 26

"Stillness was God's first language. Anything after that is a poor imitation."

Thomas Merton

Be still and know that I am God: Psalm 46:10,

How much still time is in your life, what does your phone tell you about idle time that could be transitioned to being still?

April 27

"Kindness is the language which the deaf can hear and the blind can see"

Mark Twain

This week, focus on being kind. Journal or jot down how people react to your kindness.

April 28

"Great power requires great character if it is to be a blessing and not a curse, and that character is something we only grow toward."

Dallas Willard

In our sin nature, character is not natural for us. With much that is given, much is expected. Are you building character in your life? Where are you drawing from to build that character?

April 29

> "Satan says: Look at your sin, God says: Look at my Son."
>
> *Unknown*

We are made perfect in Christ's sacrifice, Satan wants us to turn our back to that. How are you keeping your focus on Jesus?

April 30

> "But blessed is the one who trusts in the LORD, whose confidence
> is in him. They will be like a tree planted by the water that sends
> out its roots by the stream. It does not fear when heat comes; its
> leaves are always green. It has no worries in a year of drought
> and never fails to bear fruit."
>
> *Jeremiah 17:7-8*

Take inventory of where your roots are planted. Are they on barren land or
next to a stream bearing fruit?

May

May 1

"The beauty of life is,

while we cannot undo what is done,

we can see it,

understand it,

learn from it and change.

So that every new moment

is spent not in regret,

guilt,

fear or anger,

but in wisdom,

understanding and love."

Jennifer Edwards

Christ does not see your transgressions as a follower. He expects us to fall. What are you learning from your transgressions and how are you changing because of them?

May 2

"By three methods we may learn wisdom: First, by reflection, which is noblest; Second, by imitation, which is easiest; and third by experience, which is the bitterest."

Confucius

Take today and reflect on your life experiences. Do you like what you see? Write down your thoughts and review them over the next week.

May 3

"Be still, and know that I am God."

Psalm 46:10

Take a sabbath day, shut your phone and TV off and be still.

May 4

> "Do not take advantage of the widow or the fatherless. If you do and they cry out to me, I will certainly hear their cry."
>
> *Exodus 22:22*

One of our great commissions to take care of the widows and orphans. Are you ministering to them and if not, how can you engage?

May 5

> "Dear God – Thank you for not allowing me to become who I
> would've been if it was left up to me."
>
> *Unknown*

Where have you experienced God's grace today?

May 6

> "In stressful times – Seek God
>
> In painful times – Praise God
>
> In terrible times – Trust God
>
> At all times – Thank God"
>
> *Ann Voskamp*

Is God the center of your life? Today, give thanks in all circumstances to Him.

May 7

"Do not pray for easy lives. Pray to be stronger men."

John F. Kennedy

Pray today to be stronger in Him who made you. Ask Him be His light in times of adversity so those around you can see Him who is in you.

May 8

"If God is your partner, make your plans BIG!"

D.L. Moody

What BIG plan do you want to ask God to partner with you? Your God-sized deram. Does it scare you? If not, it may not be big enough.

May 9

"Whether married or single, there's only one recipe for joy in the next season of life: to seek the face of Jesus."

Dennis P. Kimbro

Look for Jesus in others. What affect does it have on your day?

May 10

"Family love, especially from such an innocent heart, is truly a Great Thought!"

Unknown

As you go through your day, search out the children and just enjoy their energy and innocence. You won't be able to not smile.

May 11

"Be watchful, stand firm in the faith, act like men, be strong. Let all that you do be done in love."

1 Corinthians 16:13-14

Act like men, be strong and do all in love? Doesn't sound so easy, does it? Try it today, see what happens.

May 12

"Speak less than you know; have more than you show."
William Shakespeare

To steal a line from Hamilton, Talk less, smile more today.

May 13

> "Courage is the first of human qualities because it is the quality which guarantees all others."
>
> *Winston Churchill*

Where do you need to be more courageous in your life? How about courageously addressing that issue - today?

May 14

> "Only madmen and fools are pleased with themselves; no wise
> man is good enough for his own satisfaction."
>
> *Benjamin Whichcote*

Let's be honest with ourselves. Where in your life do you think you don't
need Jesus? Where do you need to grow, reinvent and change? Because
you are not a madman or a fool, right?

May 15

> "Age is of no importance unless you're a cheese."
>
> *Billie Burke*

Add wisdom that comes from the Holy Spirit, does age matter?

May 16

"For this very reason do your best to add goodness to your faith; to your goodness add knowledge; to your knowledge add self-control; to your self-control add endurance; to your endurance add godliness; to your godliness add Christian affection; and to your Christian affection add love. These are the qualities you need, and if you have them in abundance, they will make you active and effective in your knowledge of our Lord Jesus Christ."

2 Peter 1:5-8 GNB

Apply this spiritual discipline to your day over the next week, look back in a week and see if you have grown in your knowledge and relationship with Jesus.

May 17

"Religion that God our Father accepts as pure and faultless is this: to look after orphans and widows in their distress."

James 1:27

Look back to May 4th and our passage from Exodus and our commission and challenge. How are you doing? If you are like me, there is some need to adjust.

May 18

> "Friendship with one's self is all important, because without it one cannot be friends with anyone else in the world."
>
> *Eleanor Roosevelt*

Another way to put this is who are you in Jesus' eyes? How will this change the way you are friends to others?

May 19

"You cannot discover new oceans until you have the courage to lose sight of the shoreline."

Anonymous

Today, what idol do you need to let go of to grow in your faith?

May 20

> "Optimism is the faith that leads to achievement. Nothing can be done without hope and confidence."
>
> *Helen Keller*

How does the confidence you have in your hope lead you in your daily life?

May 21

"Change your thoughts and you change your world"

Norman Vincent Peale

Do you have a growth mindset or a fixed mindset? To live a rich, rewarding, purposeful life, commit to learning and growing. Ingest great throughts. As you do, you'll change your life and the world.

May 22

> "I'm all for getting together with men and women in small groups around Scripture and letting it just wash over us, but for me, I've been meeting with the same ten guys for like 15 years now, but we don't have a Bible study every Friday, we have a Bible doing."
>
> *Bob Goff*

Has the spirit led you to service lately? This weekend pick one place you can serve and give back. Maybe think back to the widows and orphans, or another cause that breaks your heart. Is there something you can plug into where your service can make a difference?

May 23

> "We rarely ever see the full spectrum of God's plan, and our simple deeds can spiral into much bigger blessings."
>
> *Delilah*

Reflect on May 16, one week ago, has your discipline and simple deeds spiraled into much more?

May 24

> "I must not fear. Fear is the mind-killer. Fear is the little-death that brings total obliteration. I will face my fear. I will permit it to pass over me and through me. And when it has gone past I will turn the inner eye to see its path. Where the fear has gone there will be nothing. Only I will remain."
>
> *Fran Herbert (Dune Chronicles #1)*

Today examine your fears. What are they? What are they rooted in? Name them. Think about how the are affecting you and what you can do to minimize - and obliterate - those fears.

May 25

"After a busy, seemingly dreary day I went outside and the sun
burst out with a glorious brightness. A reminder that God is always
at hand whether seen or unseen, it felt like he was waiting for me
to come outside and He just wanted to remind me he is ever
present!"

Unknown

Enjoy today and bask in the beauty of God's creation. Take note of all you
see and reflect on it at the end of the day in your journal.

May 26

8 THINGS TO REMEMBER WHEN GOING THROUGH TOUGH TIMES

1. Everything can – and will – change.

2. You've overcome challenges before.

3. It's a learning experience.

4. Not getting what you want can be a blessing.

5. Allow yourself to have some fun.

6. Being kind to your self is the best medicine.

7. Other people's negativity isn't worth worrying about.

8. And there is always, always, always something to be thankful for!

Unknown

Gratitude is the cure for a lot of ailments. In times of frustration or self doubt, take a couple of minutes to write down some things you are grateful for and notice how that renews your mind. Remember the gratitude journal routine shared on February 6? If you aren't doing it, give it a try.

May 27

"Give thanks in all circumstances; for this is God's will for you in
Christ Jesus."

1 Thessalonians 5:18

Reflect back on yesterday's list of things you are grateful for and give a
prayer of thanks.

May 28

"Money is not required to buy one necessity of the soul."

Thoreau

What does your soul need today? Has it been a long week and does it need rest? Has it been anxious and does it need joy? Take some time to invest into your soul today. It doesn't cost anything but has a great value.

May 29

> "This is good for a weekend: So whether you eat or drink, or whatever you do, do it all for the Glory of God."
>
> *1 Cor 10:31*

Decide now what you will do this weekend to glorify the Lord. Spend time with Him, volunteer, serve others?

May 30

> "Though no one can go back and make a brand new start,
> anyone can start from now and make a brand new ending."
>
> *Carl Bard*

Look back at your mistakes, your sin. Give it to God and repent to Him. Then let it go, turn your back to it and move forward giving thanks to Him.

May 31

> "Nobody, absolutely nobody, is beyond God's reach."
>
> *Jim Maxim*

Remember the parable of the Prodigal Son. Who do you know who is suffering and needs some loving encouragement?

June

June 1

> "Never underestimate the ability of a small group of committed individuals to change the world."
>
> *Margaret Mead*

This book was written by a small group that came together to build each other up. Review the bios of the individuals who came to put this book together. Do you think this small group has impacted the world? Has this small group impacted you?

June 2

> "Strong lives are motivated by dynamic purposes."
>
> *Kenneth Hildebrand*

Look back again at the bios of the people who contributed to this book. Each has a purpose statement. How is that purpose statement causing them to act? What is your purpose statement? How do you act on it? Write it down and share it with your closest friends.

June 3

> "Every creature is a book about God."
>
> *Meister Eckhart*

Take five people you encounter today and write down where you see God in them. Share it with them after you reflect on it tonight.

June 4

"The richest man is not he who has the most, but he who needs the least."

Unknown

Do you believe that less is more? Less clutter, less business, less fear mean more peace, joy and love? Ponder how this could be true in your life. What's one thing you could do to de-clutter, starting today?

June 5

"Life is a Gift, not a Given."

Hallmark card

Give thanks to God today for the gift you have been given. Take some
time this weekend to show Him how thankful you are.

June 6

"Life without risk is like no life at all!"

Unknown

Step out of your comfort zone today with your commitment and actions.
How does it feel? How did ou grow?

June 7

"Our hearts are restless until they rest in God."

St. Augustine

Today, read Psalms for 15 minutes. What is your take away from your reading regarding peace and rest?

June 8

> "The antidote to exhaustion is not necessarily rest. The antidote to exhaustion is wholeheartedness."
>
> *David Whyte, Crossing the Unknown Sea Work as a Pilgrimage of Identity*

What does wholeheartedness mean to you? Does it bring you rest? Is there purpose in your wholeheartedness? Is there gratitude? Is there identity in our Creator there?

June 9

> "I don't focus on what I'm up against. I focus on my goals and I try to ignore the rest."
>
> *Venus Williams*

Goals are good but are they idols or something to help keep focus on a greater purpose?

June 10

"We must let go of the life we have planned, so as to accept the life that is waiting for us."

Joseph Campbell

Include God in your planning for today. See what surprises He has in store for you. As you prepare to retire for the night, look back on how it unfolded.

June 11

> "Worry does not empty tomorrow of its sorrows; it empties today of its strength."
>
> *Corrie Ten Boom*

Pray for His strength today, to see how He sees things, to hear how He hears things and to speak the words He wants you to speak.

June 12

"Always plan ahead. It wasn't raining when Noah built the ark."

Richard Cushing

It was God's prompting to Noah to build the ark. Have you looked for God's prompting in your plans?

June 13

> "I don't think of all the misery, but of the beauty that still remains."
>
> *Ann Frank*

Joy comes from a place of gratitude. Ann Frank renewed her mind to live in the present and not the past. If you are holding onto something in the past, renew and turn toward the future. Look toward the future with optimism and hope, knowing God has great plans for you.

"Give thanks to the LORD, for he is good; his love endures forever. Let Israel say: "His love endures forever." Let the house of Aaron say: "His love endures forever." Let those who fear the LORD say: "His love endures forever." When hard pressed, I cried to the LORD; he brought me into a spacious place. The LORD is with me; I will not be afraid. What can mere mortals do to me? The LORD is with me; he is my helper. I look in triumph on my enemies. It is better to take refuge in the LORD than to trust in humans. It is better to take refuge in the LORD than to trust in princes. All the nations surrounded me, but in the name of the LORD I cut them down. They surrounded me on every side, but in the name of the LORD I cut them down. They swarmed around me like bees, but they were consumed as quickly as burning thorns; in the name of the LORD I cut them down. I was pushed back and about to fall, but the LORD helped me. The LORD is my strength and my defense ; he has become my salvation. Shouts of joy and victory resound in the tents of the righteous: "The LORD's right hand has done mighty things! The LORD's right hand is lifted high; the LORD's right hand has done mighty things!" I will not die but live, and will proclaim what the LORD has done. The LORD has chastened me severely, but he has not given me over to death."

Psalm 118:1-18

Reflect on verse 14: The Lord is my strength and my defense; he has become my salvation. Through trials and being chastened, you come to know the Lord's presence with you and you learn to trust and He becomes your salvation in your heart. Think about your story of how Christ is becoming or has become your salvation.

> "Never underestimate the valuable and important difference you make in every life you touch, for the impact you make today has a powerful rippling effect on every tomorrow."
>
> *Anonymous*

Do you know that even an introvered "regular" person will influence over 10,000 people over a lifetime? As we enter the week before father's day, if you are a parent, an aunt or uncle or a mentor, this is a great perspective that we are planting seeds and we don't know exactly how they will grow, what they will produce and who all it will feed. Who will you impact?

June 16

"Alone we can do so little; together we can do so much."

Helen Keller

Do you have a partner in doing? If you do, thank them for their partnership today. If not, make a list of people you'd like to do life with. Hint: We're partial to the SAM methodology as described in our story.

June 17

> "It is easier to build strong children than to repair broken men."
>
> *Frederick Douglas*

Some good advice I received was to have the perspective that I was the parent and I have the responsibility to not do something that puts me first and hurts our children for a lifetime. Be careful of your words and actions with children. It is too often the father who scars the heart of his children. If you've made a mistake, discuss with your child. Encourage them to share their experience. Listen carefully. Apologize and commit to operating differently in the future. Pray for strength and guidance. No one is perfect, but committing to these steps, when you have hurt your child with words, can be a pathway to a better tomorrow in your relationship.

June 18

"Being a dad means learning the fine art of letting go."
Unknown

Teaching your childern to live without you is hard. Where is holding on in your life not letting someone else flourish?

June 19

> "Being a dad means teaching your kids that they can be an instrument of God by helping those less fortunate."
>
> *Unknown*

Being a dad, made in Christ's image, acting as Christ has taught us, is a powerful example to your children. What can you do now to show your children it's not about you, but about Christ's kingdom?

June 20

"Being a dad means raising your kids to live without you."

Unknown

Reflect on how you have let go and truly turned your children over to God's heavenly care?

June 21

> "Being a dad means praying for guidance. Daily."
>
> *Unknown*

What guidance do you need as a parent? Ask God for his guidance and act on what He has revealed to you.

June 22

> "Being a dad means being trusted with the biggest responsibility imaginable: raising His child. And remembering He is right by your side each step of the way."
>
> *Unknown*

Today, look back on Father's Day. What are you grateful for and where did you see God in that?

June 23

> "If you put off everything till you're sure of it, you'll never get anything done."
>
> *Norman Vincent Peale*

Are you like me and get paralysis by analysis sometimes? Today, ask for God's direction and follow His prompting and move forward.

June 24

"Time has a way of showing us what is important in life." Had some time to reflect and reach out to a few people today and reminded me to stop and reach out to those who are important to us!

Unknown

Reach out to someone today that you haven't talked to for at least a year. Call them. Let them know you are thinking of them. It's amazing what can happen.

June 25

"If you don't like something, change it. If you can't change it, change the way you think about it."

Mary Engelbreit

I bet there is something reoccuring in your life that you'd really like to have different. Can it be changed? Reflect and write down at least three ways you can address it with a different thought process.

June 26

"Leadership in action, not position: It's not the lions roar that signals danger. It's their silence"

Unknown

In what ways do you lead? Do you make people better by the way you serve them? That is kingdom building. Adjust your leadership style as necessary. Thank God for your gifts today.

June 27

"Every day, I like getting up because there's another challenge"

Roger Penske

Are you taking on the day as a challenge worth getting up for or are you letting it overcome you? What great purpose or cause will you embrace today? Who will you dedicate the day to?

June 28

> "All this is for your benefit, so that the grace that is reaching more and more people may cause thanksgiving to overflow to the glory of God. Therefore we do not lose heart. Though outwardly we are wasting away, yet inwardly we are being renewed day by day"
>
> *2 Corinthians 4:15-16*

Even thought your outward body may be getting weaker and more frail, reflect on how you could benefit from the inward renewing of your heart and mind. You can grow heart and mind until your final day on earth. Where can you give thanksgiving today that gives God all the glory?

June 29

> "Failure is success if we learn from it."
>
> *Malcolm S. Forbes*

Think back to where you did not succeed in something. Has it made you better or have you avoided those situations again? Should you be applying the lessons you learned in a different way? Are you better at being you because of those failures?

June 30

> "Gratitude unlocks the fullness of life"
>
> *Melody Beattie*

Give thanks in all circumstances, where do you need to give thanks today that may be causing stress?

July

July 1

> "You never know how strong you are until being strong is your only choice."
>
> *Bob Marley*

What do you need to take a stand on today?

July 2

> "Remember who you are. Don't compromise for anyone, for any reason. You are a child of the Almighty God. Live that truth."
>
> *Lysa Terkeurst*

Where do you need to be strong this week?

July 3

> "Many of life's failures are experienced by people who did not realize how close they were to success when they gave up."
>
> *Thomas Edison*

The easy path is easy for a reason - it does not meet your potential. Where do you need to buckle down to drive to something great?

July 4

"As we express our gratitude, we must never forget that the highest appreciation is not to utter words but to live by them."

John F. Kennedy

How are you being honorable on the anniversary of our country's freedom?

July 5

"The story of your life is the story of the journey of your heart through a dangerous and beautiful world. It is a story of the long and sustained assault on your heart by the enemy who knows who you could be and fears you."

John Eldredge

Believe in yourself as you mean more to so many people than you even realize. Where can you step forward to be the change?

July 6

"Life every man holds dear; but the dear man holds honor far more precious dear than life."

William Shakespeare

Where might you need to take an honorable stand?

July 7

"Life is not a problem to be solved, it is an adventure to be lived."
John Eldredge

What is your next adventure?

July 8

"Continuous effort -- not strength nor intelligence -- is the key to unlocking our potential."

Winston Churchill

Where are you frustrated with how something is going, and can you approach it in a new way?

July 9

"Don't judge each day by the harvest you reap but by the seeds that you plant."

Robert Louis Stevenson

Where can you plant seeds today in hopes of bearing fruit?

July 10

> "People who cannot invent and reinvent themselves must be content with borrowed postures, secondhand ideas, fitting in instead of standing out."
>
> *Warren Bennis*

In what areas of your life must you reinvent? Think of the eight key ares of life: faith, partner/spouse, family, work, health and fitness, finances, friends and fun. How would you rate your current satisfaction on a scale of 1 - 10 for each key area? That should give you some clues on where you must grow, reinvent and change.

July 11

> "I am better off healed than I ever was unbroken."
>
> *Beth Moore*

What has hurt you recently and what can you learn from it?

July 12

"God will meet you where you are in order to take you where He wants you to go."

Tony Evans

Now is the time and place to accept God has a plan for you. Remember that your journey starts with a first step on roads that may extend far beyond your site. God's grace is the same in that wherever you are he still loves you and wants to guide you.

July 13

> "Our greatest fear should not be of failure but of succeeding at things in life that don't really matter."
>
> *Francis Chan*

What is your purpose and in 20 years will it matter?

July 14

> "Saying you believe in yourself will not guarantee your success,
> but saying you DO NOT believe in yourself will guarantee failure"
>
> *John Maxwell*

How do you walk out of your door in the morning - shuffling along or with a confident step forward? Believe in yourself today, you will do great things!

July 15

> "I learned that courage was not the absence of fear, but the triumph over it. The brave man is not he who does not feel afraid, but he who conquers that fear."
>
> *Nelson Mandela*

Everyone needs fear. What are you afraid of and how will you deal with it?

July 16

"Have you prayed about it as much as you've talked about it?"
Matthew 21:22

Can you spend time today to both come to God and listen for his response?

July 17

> "I am not a product of my circumstances. I am a product of my decisions."
>
> *Stephen Covey*

Realize you always have a choice. What's the most important decision you need to make in your life currently?

July 18

"Our thoughts, not our circumstances, determine our happiness."
John Maxwell

Life is full of perspective. Are you focusing on the perspective which gives the best you for the situation?

July 19

"We never grow closer to God when we just live life. It takes deliberate pursuit and attentiveness."

Francis Chan

Are you stuck in a rut in your faith? God would love to have a conversation when you take the time to talk with Him.

"Humility is not thinking less of yourself; it is thinking of yourself less."
Rick Warren

How are you lifting others up today?

July 21

> "Keep up or step aside. My goals won't let me slow down!"
>
> *Brad Lea*

Ask for and expect much from people, but also don't hesitate in bringing them forward with you.

July 22

> "Your word is a lamp unto my feet, and a light unto my path."
>
> *Psalms 119:105*

Are you open to listening to guidance to guide you forward in your path?

July 23

> "To that one soul reading this. I know you're tired, you're fed up, you're close to breaking but there's strength within you, even when you feel weak. KEEP FIGHTING!"
>
> *Power of Positivity*

Know that you've got this and start small - what can you check off your list as done today?

July 24

> "You may not know what you are going to do; you only know that God knows what he is going to do."
>
> *Oswald Chambers*

Have you asked God to lead you yet today?

July 25

"Excellence is not a gift, but a skill that takes practice. We do not act 'rightly' because we are 'excellent', in fact we achieve 'excellence' by acting 'rightly.'"

Plato

Where should you be focusing on core values this week?

July 26

> "Pray like it depends on God. Work like it depends on you."
>
> *Mark Batterson, Play the Man (The 5th virtue of Manhood: True Grit)*

Where are you asking God for help while driving the path forward?

July 27

> "Decisions you repeat will form the life you lead"
>
> *Levi Lusko*

There are always issues requiring your time. Don't be afraid to step back and say 'will this matter a year or five years from now'. If not, is it worth you shorting other things now?

July 28

"Everyone has a plan until they get punched in the face."

Mike Tyson

Do you need to throw your plan out and accept that a change will help you?

July 29

"More men fail through lack of purpose than lack of talent."
Billy Sunday

What are you driving toward?

July 30

"The only disability in life is a bad attitude."

Scott Hamilton

Is there someone or something you are dealing with that may need your grace?

July 31

> "Those who sow in tears shall reap with joyful shouting"
>
> *Psalms 126:5*

To find the plentiful outcome often takes frustration and pains. Where do you need to accept the frustration and tears on your path?

August

August 1

> "I've missed more than nine thousand shots in my career. I've lost almost three hundred games. Twenty-six times I've been trusted to make the game winning shot and missed. I've failed over and over and over again in my life. And that is why I succeed".
>
> *Michael Jordan*

Where have you failed and leaned from it recently?

August 2

> "The most important aspect of Christianity is not the work we do, but the relationship we maintain and the surrounding influence and qualities produced by that relationship. That is all God asks us to give our attention to, and it is the one thing that is continually under attack."
>
> *Oswald Chambers*

How can you focus on relationships today - both with God and others?

August 3

"I believe in the possible. I believe, small though we are, insignificant though we may be, we can reach a full understanding of the universe. You were right when you said you felt small, looking up at all that up there. We are very, very small, but we are profoundly capable of very, very big things."

Stephen Hawking

Go beyond your expectations - where else are you going to make a difference today?

August 4

"If God called us to a task, He will then qualify us for the job."

Jack Hyle

The God who spoke being into existence is leading you to something outside your comfort zone. Step forward because He has your back and you can do this! What is stopping you that God can't handle?

August 5

"I would prefer even to fail with honor than win by cheating."

Sophocles

Short term gains of unscrupulous wins will lead to lifetime regrets of how things may have been.

August 6

> "If God's love for his children is to be measured by our health, wealth, and comfort, then God hated the Apostle Paul."
>
> *John Piper*

God still loves us in times of struggle. Is there someone you know who is struggling that you can come beside to remind them how much God still loves them?

August 7

> "A river cuts through a rock not because of its power, but its persistence."
>
> *Unknown*

Are you continuing to work toward your purpose and goals this week with a fierce devotion?

August 8

> "We can't help everyone, but everyone can help someone."
>
> *Ronald Reagan*

Who in your life could use a phone call, a meeting for coffee, or a helping hand today?

August 9

"God loves us more than we will ever know and cares for us in
ways we will never fully understand."

William M. Sliva

How can you give thanks to God today for all the blessings He gives?

August 10

"One day or Day one, you decide."

Paulo Coelho

How can you take that first step on your new adventure?

August 11

> "The bad news: Time flies. The good news: You're the pilot!"
>
> *Mark Lachs*

Are you using your time as the most precious resource this week? You should be.

August 12

"The will of God will not take us where the grace of God cannot sustain us."

Billy Graham

Do you feel frustrated today and challenging yourself on whether this is actually God's plan for you? God WILL sustain you and he DOES have a plan for you!

August 13

> "I will lead the blind by ways they have not known, along unfamiliar paths I will guide them."
>
> *Isaiah 42:16*

Is there something you need to hand over to God today?

August 14

> "Tolerance isn't about not having beliefs. It's about how your beliefs lead you to treat people who disagree with you."
>
> *Tim Keller*

Do you have an opportunity this week to lead by example in dealing with people who disagree with you?

August 15

> "Above all be of single aim; have a legitimate and useful purpose, and devote yourself unreservedly to it."
>
> *James Allen*

Once again, what is your life's purpose?

August 16

"The greater your knowledge of the goodness and grace of God on your life, the more likely you are to praise Him in the storm."

Matt Chandler

Who do you know who is struggling right now who may need a reminder of God's love for them?

August 17

"Words can inspire, thoughts can provoke, but only action truly brings you closer to your dreams."

Brad Sugars

What can you move from talking to doing today? Take that step!

August 18

> "God loves each of us as if there were only one of us"
>
> *Saint Augustine*

Do you ever feel small in a big world? Remember that our God takes time to make every snowflake which has ever come to be different from all of the others, and don't you think he loves you more than that? You are YOU - celebrate it and celebrate God's love.

August 19

"Never mistake motion for action."

Ernest Hemingway

Are you spending energy on the root causes of your opportunity or problem? Where are you falling victim to process problems? Or where to you suffer from a lack of focus? How will you get yourself beyond that noise today?

August 20

> "Remember who you are. Don't compromise for anyone, for any reason. You are a child of the Almighty God. Live that truth."
>
> *Lysa TerKeurst*

Is there anywhere you need to stand up for yourself or others this week?

August 21

> "The great use of life is to spend it for something that will outlast it."
>
> *William James*

What will be your legacy?

August 22

"What you do has greater impact than what you say."
Stephen Covey

What do you need to take the first step on your new path?

August 23

> "For it is by grace you have been saved, through faith—and this is not from yourselves, it is the gift of God"
>
> *Ephesians 2:8*

Jesus is God's ultimate sacrifice for us to give us grace. Who are we to hold grace back from others. Is there anyone you need to extend grace to this week?

August 24

"Life is either a daring adventure or it is nothing at all."
Helen Keller

How are you stepping out of your comfort-zone this week?

August 25

> "Success is nothing more than a few simple disciplines, practiced every day; while failure is simply a few errors in judgment, repeated every day. It is the accumulative weight of our disciplines and our judgments that leads us to either fortune or failure."
>
> *Jim Rohn*

Are you learning from your errors or constraining yourself to repeat them? Success leaves clues. You can be more - strive to be the best every day.

August 26

> "Trust the past to God's mercy, the present to God's love, and the future to God's providence."
>
> *Augustine*

Are there areas of your life you need to accept God is in control?

August 27

"Live as if you'll die tomorrow. Learn as if you'll live forever."
Gandhi

How can you be a better you today?

August 28

> "Small deeds done are better than great deeds planned."
>
> *Peter Marshall*

Where can you move to action today? What taks can you complete today?

August 29

"Travel makes one modest. You see what a tiny place you occupy in the world."

Gustave Flaubert

There is so much of the world to see and experience. How are you broadening yourself this week? What new experiences are you planning?

August 30

"May the Lord answer you in the day of trouble! The name of the God of Jacob protect you! May he send you help from the sanctuary and support from Zion!"

Psalms 20

What is troubling you this week? Have you turned it over to God?

August 31

"Nothing is impossible. The word itself says 'I'm possible.'"

Audrey Hepburn

Think back to ideas you have written off. Why not chase the absurd one?
Even if it fails, the perspective you'll have will set you up perfectly for your
next venture.

September

September 1

> "The most difficult thing is the decision to act, the rest is merely tenacity."
>
> *Amelia Earhart*

What is the first step on your new path?

September 2

> "You're only here for a short visit. Don't hurry, don't worry. And be sure to smell the flowers along the way."
>
> *Walter Hagen*

Where do you need to step back and take a breath this week? It will be worth it!

September 3

> "If opportunity doesn't knock, build a door"
>
> *Milton Bearle*

If you've identified your purpose, what do you need to get things going?
Once you start moving just stay with it. What are you chasing right now?

September 4

> "'Be a Blessing.' Three simple words, but what a profound impact we experience when we act on them."
>
> *Debbie Macomber*

What are you doing to be a blessing today?

September 5

> "Success is not measured in the amount of dollars you make, but the amount of lives you impact."
>
> *Anonymous*

Are you working on something bigger than you? You can and must!

September 6

> "Pride goes before destruction, a haughty spirit before a fall."
>
> *Proverbs 16:18*

Are your great deeds this week yours or were they given to you by a loving God?

September 7

> "Start by doing what's necessary; then do what's possible; and suddenly you are doing the impossible."
>
> *Francis of Assisi*

On this Labor Day, think of how you are challenging yourself daily to broaden your view?

September 8

> "I truly believe that no one can close the door that God has opened to you."
>
> *Ciara*

What is the door God is opening for you? There will always be people with opinions saying "don't go that way" - don't be afraid to say "thank you for your input" and jump into that open door!

September 9

> "The expert in anything was once a beginner."
>
> *Helen Hayes*

Where do you need to get out and try?

September 10

"Focus on your feet, not your head. Keep them moving forward!"

Jen Welter (first woman NFL coach)

Are you advancing down the field or waiting for the ref to call a timeout?
You can do more!

September 11

"Don't waste your life in doubts and fears: spend yourself on the work before you, well assured that the right performance of this hour's duties will be the best preparation for the hours or ages that follow it."

Ralph Waldo Emerson

As we remember a tradgedy on this date, focus on looking forward to make the most of your life. How can you move from fears to action this week?

September 12

"Failure is success in progress."

Albert Einstein

What have you tried differently today?

September 13

"My life purpose is to 'do something for God'. Until he says stop, I'll keep going."

Dolly Parton

What are you chasing that is 'bigger than you'?

September 14

"Whether you think you can or think you can't you're right."
Henry Ford

How are you believing in yourself today?

"Your children are not your children.

They are sons and daughters of Life's longing for itself.

They come through you but not from you.

And though they are with you yet they belong not to you.

You may give them your love but not your thoughts,

For they have their own thoughts.

You may house their bodies but not their souls,

For their souls dwell in the house of tomorrow, which you cannot visit, not even in your dreams.

You may strive to be like them, but seek not to make them like you.

For life goes not backward nor tarries with yesterday.

You are the bows from which your children as living arrows are sent forth.

The archer sees the make upon the path of the infinite, and He bends you with His might that His arrows may go swift and far.

Let your bending in the archer's hand be for gladness.

For even as He loves the arrow that flies, so He also loves the bow that is stable."

Kahlil Gibran

What are you doing to make the next generation better than yours?

September 16

"God is most glorified in us when we are most satisfied in Him"
John Piper

Have you taken time to both talk and listen with God lately?

September 17

> "Everybody is a genius. But if you judge a fish by its ability to climb
> a tree, it will live its whole life believing that it is stupid."
>
> *Albert Einstein*

Who might you have accidentally judged or looked at using
preconceptions and potentially the wrong measuring stick? Where can you
broaden your perspective today?

September 18

"Happy are those whose greatest desire is to do what God requires; God will satisfy them fully!"

Matthew 5:6

Have you allowed God to help you define your purpose?

September 19

> "Success comes when you do what you love to do, and commit to being the best in your field."
>
> *Brian Tracy*

Why accept anything less than being the best?

"If you want to be truly happy, you won't find it on an endless quest for more stuff. You'll find it in receiving God's generosity and then passing that generosity along."

Bill Hybels

Generosity is much more than just money or time - how can you be generous today?

September 21

> "Don't let what you cannot do interfere with what you can do."
> *John Wooden*

Believe in yourself. You can do it. Now buckle down and make it work!

September 22

"Associate yourself with people of good quality, for it is better to be alone than in bad company."

Booker T Washington

Who are the non-relatives you call your brothers or sisters?

September 23

> "Do not let unwholesome talk come out of your mouths, but only what is helpful for building others up according to their needs, that it may benefit those who listen."
>
> *Ephesians 4:29*

How can you model the best version of your Father's you today?

September 24

> "I am able to do all things through Him who strengthens me."
> *Philippians 4:13*

What are you fearful of today? Have you asked God to help you be strong for it?

September 25

> "Between stimulus and response, there is a space. In that space is our power to choose our response. In our response lies our growth and our freedom."
>
> *Viktor E. Frankl*

Have you allowed space and thought to overcome emotional responses or are you allowing emotions to carry the day?

September 26

> "A life spent making mistakes is not only more honorable, but more useful than a life spent doing nothing."
>
> *George Bernard Shaw*

Get up, get out, and go try today!

September 27

"God has raised from death our Lord Jesus, who is the Great Shepherd of the sheep as the result of his blood, by which the eternal covenant is sealed. May the God of peace provide you with every good thing you need in order to do his will, and may he, through Jesus Christ, do in us what pleases him. And to Christ be the glory for ever and ever! Amen."

Hebrews 13:20-21

How will you glorify God today?

September 28

> "Scared is what you're feeling. Brave is what you're doing."
>
> *Emma Donoghue*

How can you get out there and blaze a trail this week?

September 29

> "Life is wasted if we do not grasp the glory of the cross, cherish it for the treasure that it is, and cleave to it as the highest price of every pleasure and the deepest comfort in every pain. What was once foolishness to us-a crucified God-must become our wisdom and our power and our only boast in this world."
>
> *John Piper*

Is there someone God calls you to share with today? What an unbelievable gift we have been given in Christ Jesus.

September 30

> "The hard days are the best because that's where champions are made."
>
> *Gabby Douglas*

Think of both wins and losses in the last week - how can you respond to stressors to achieve more wins?

October

October 1

"Never give your family the leftovers and crumbs of your time."
Charles Swindoll

What are you prioritizing above family and how can you change that?

"Friendship Points to the Meaning of the Universe:

Friendship points to the ultimate end of our existence. God doesn't just forgive us through Christ; he befriends us (John 15:13–15). He saves us to glorify him by enjoying fellowship with him forever. We are headed toward an eternal world of fellowship — with God and with all whom he's befriended through Christ.

Friendship is also the means to this end, because the cross is the most heroic act of friendship history has ever known. Jesus said, "Greater love has no one than this, that someone lay down his life for his friends" (John 15:13). The cross is the greatest expression of love, and Jesus wants us to understand it as a sacrifice for friends. The single greatest moment in history, where we see God's glory shine most brightly, is this cosmic act of friendship."

Pastor Drew Hunter, writing on the value of Friendship:

In what way can you love a friend sacrificially?

October 3

> "I have given God a million reasons not to love me. None of them changed his mind!"
>
> *Paul Washer*

What sin can you place under the Blood of Christ today, so that you can emerge healed?

October 4

"Integrity is more valuable than income. Honor is richer than fame. Self-worth is wealthier than net worth."

Robin Sharma

What changes do you need to make in your life to deepen your integrity?

October 5

> "The day we find the perfect church, it becomes imperfect the moment we join it."
>
> *Charles H. Spurgeon*

Am I setting myself up for disappointment by expecting my church to be perfect?

October 6

"One of the greatest tragedies in life is to lose your own sense of self and accept the version of you that is expected by everyone else."

K.L. Toth

How might you be limiting yourself and what can you do to change that?

October 7

"Do not love the world nor the things in the world. If anyone loves the world, the love of the Father is not in him. For all that is in the world, the lust of the flesh and the lust of the eyes and the boastful pride of life, is not from the Father, but is from the world. The world is passing away, and also its lusts; but the one who does the will of God lives forever."

1 John 2:15-17

What worthless trinket is the world dangling in front of your eyes? Pray to be released from it.

October 8

"Any gift from God used rightly is an ally to our joy in God, but they can become our joy, rather than God. If you are on guard against only bad things, you are asleep to half the battle. For many of us, the greatest danger comes from good things we can't let go of."

John Piper

What are the good things in my life that have become an idol to me, that when I look at them, if lost would damage my relationship with God?

October 9

> "My mission in life is not merely to survive, but to thrive; and to do so with some passion, some compassion, some humor, and some style."
>
> *Maya Angelou*

Which of these attributes do you want to have increased in your life? Thriving? Passion? Compassion? Humor? Style? Lift up your request in prayer.

"Beware of destination addiction: a preoccupation with the idea that happiness is found in the next place, the next job, or with the next partner. Until you give up that idea that happiness is somewhere else, it will never be where you are.

As an antidote to Destination Addiction, meditate on Philippians 4:11-13:

Actually, I don't have a sense of needing anything personally. I've learned by now to be quite content whatever my circumstances. I'm just as happy with little as with much, with much as with little. I've found the recipe for being happy whether full or hungry, hands full or hands empty. Whatever I have, wherever I am, I can make it through anything in the One who makes me who I am."

Robert Holden, Philippians 4:11-13

What fantasy regarding a place, a job, or a partner do you need to toss out of your life before it derails your walk with the Lord?

October 11

> "Let us hold tightly without wavering to the hope we affirm, for God can be trusted to keep his promise. Let us think of ways to motivate one another to acts of love and good works. And let us not neglect our meeting together, as some people do, but encourage one another, especially now that the day of Christ's return is drawing near."
>
> *Hebrews 10: 23-25*

Have you found a group of like-minded believers with whom you can do life?

October 12

A six-year old's view on why dogs live shorter lives than people:

"People are born so that they can learn how to live a good life –
like loving everybody all the time and being nice."

"Dogs already know how to do that so they don't have to stay for
as long as we do!"

Live simply

Love generously

Care deeply

Speak kindly

VetWest Animal Hospitals

What characteristics from a dog's manner of living can you apply in your
life today?

October 13

"What you feel is what you are and what you are is beautiful."
Goo Goo Dolls

How can you embrace your inner beauty today?

October 14

> "To be yourself in a world that is constantly trying to make you something else is the greatest accomplishment."
>
> *Ralph Waldo Emerson*

What compromises with the world do you need to stop making?

October 15

"Look carefully then how you walk, not as unwise but as wise, making the best use of the time, because the days are evil. Therefore do not be foolish, but understand what the will of the Lord is. And do not get drunk with wine, for that is debauchery, but be filled with the Spirit, addressing one another in psalms and hymns and spiritual songs, singing and making melody to the Lord with your heart, giving thanks always and for everything to God the Father in the name of our Lord Jesus Christ, submitting to one another out of reverence for Christ."

EPHESIANS 5:15–21

As you ask the Holy Spirit's help in taking a spiritual inventory of your life, what are you prepared to change?

October 16

> "It doesn't make sense to hire smart people and tell them what to do; we hire smart people so they can tell us what to do."
>
> *Steve Jobs*

What smart people do you need to start associating with?

October 17

> "First, think. Second, believe. Third, dream. And finally, dare."
>
> *Walt Disney*

Where are you along this think, believe, dream, dare timeline? What's keeping you from moving to the next step?

October 18

> "We can achieve the utmost in economies by engineering knowledge; we can conquer new fields by research; we can build plants and machines that shall stand among the wonders of the world; but unless we put the right man in the right place-unless we make it possible for our workers and executives alike to enjoy a sense of satisfaction in their jobs, our efforts will have been in vain."
>
> *E.R. Stettinius, Jr.*

If you're in a leadership role of any kind, how will you increase the satisfaction and impact of your co-workers?

October 19

> "He defends the cause of the fatherless and the widow, and loves the foreigner residing among you, giving them food and clothing."
>
> *Deuteronomy 10:18*

Who is hurting in your community and how can you minister to them?

October 20

> "Discussions are always better than arguments, because an argument is to find out who is right, and a discussion is to find out what is right."
>
> *ResearchGate*

As you enter your next awkward or tense situation, how can you frame the conversation as a discussion instead of an argument?

October 21

> "So often, it's others around us who can see where God wants to grow us even before we see it ourselves."
>
> *James MacDonald, Christ-Centered Biblical Counseling: Changing Lives with God's Changeless Truth*

Ask a couple of your closest friends for their insights into how God may want you to grow.

October 22

"Love chooses to believe the best about people. It gives them the benefit of the doubt. It refuses to fill in the unknowns with negative assumptions. As much as possible, love focuses on the positive."

Stephen Kendrick

Is there a person about whom you're holding negative assumptions? How can you flip the script?

"If a dog was the teacher you would learn things like:

· When your loved one comes home always run to greet them.

· Never pass up an opportunity to go for a joyride.

· Allow the experience of fresh air and wind in your face to be pure Ecstasy.

· Take naps.

· Stretch before rising.

· Run, romp and play daily.

· Thrive on attention and let people touch you.

· Avoid biting when a simple growl will do.

· On warm days, stop to lie down on your back on the grass.

· On hot days, drink lots of water and lie under a shady tree.

· When you're happy, dance around and wag your entire body.

· Delight in the simple joy of a long walk.

· Be faithful.

· Never pretend to be something you're not.

· If what you want lies buried, dig until you find it.

· When someone is having a bad day, be silent, sit close by and nuzzle them gently.

That's the secret of happiness we can learn from a good dog!"

Anonymous

Which of these characteristics do you need to apply in your life today?

October 24

"Love is helping people toward the greatest beauty, the highest value, the deepest satisfaction, the most lasting joy, the biggest reward, the most wonderful friendship, and the most overwhelming worship — love is helping people toward God. We do this by pointing to the greatness of God. And God does it by pointing to the greatness of God."

John Piper

What one change can you make in your life that will help to point people to the greatness of God?

October 25

"Keep your eyes open and try to catch people in your company doing something right, then praise them for it."

Tom Hopkins

Which of your co-workers or friends can you affirm today?

October 26

> "Good teaching is an act of hospitality toward the young, and hospitality is always an act that benefits the host even more than the guest. The concept of hospitality arose in ancient times when this reciprocity was easier to see: in nomadic cultures, the food and shelter one gave to a stranger yesterday is the food and shelter one hopes to receive from a stranger tomorrow. By offering hospitality, one participates in the endless reweaving of a social fabric on which all can depend—thus the gift of sustenance for the guest becomes a gift of hope for the host. It is that way in teaching as well: the teacher's hospitality to the student results in a world more hospitable to the teacher."
>
> *Parker J. Palmer, The Courage to Teach: Exploring the Inner Landscape of a Teacher's Life*

Who can you bless today with hospitality?

October 27

> "We are all faced with a series of great opportunities brilliantly disguised as impossible situations."
>
> *Chuck Swindoll*

What opportunity can you find in that seemingly impossible situation?

October 28

> "Don't be afraid to start over again, this time you are not starting from scratch; you're starting from Experience!"
>
> *Biggs Burke*

What lesson or guidance can you take from a failure or setback that you've experienced in your life?

October 29

> "Gratitude turns what we have into enough, and more. It turns denial into acceptance, chaos into order, confusion into clarity...it makes sense of our past, brings peace for today, and creates a vision for tomorrow."
>
> *Melody Beattie*

What gratitude prayer will you lift up to God today?

October 30

> "You have a one-of-a-kind gift to offer this world, and you are unique in the entire history of creation."
>
> *Wayne Dyer*

What words would you use in a prayer of thanks to God for making you unique?

October 31

"I started succeeding when I started leaving small fights for small fighters. I stopped fighting those who gossiped about me... I stopped fighting with my in laws... I stopped fighting for attention... I stopped fighting to meet peoples expectation of me... I stopped fighting for my rights with inconsiderate people.. I stopped fighting to please everyone... I stopped fighting to prove they were wrong about me.... I left such fights for those who have nothing else to fight... And I started fighting for my vision, my dreams, my ideas and my destiny. The day I gave up on small fights is the day I started becoming successful & so much more content. Some fights are not worth your time..... Choose what you fight for wisely."

Kimberley Stefanski

What small fights do you need to leave behind?

November

November 1

"Your past does not belong to you.

It does not have to haunt you or hover over your mind anymore.

It belongs to God and that's why He can rewrite it as He chooses.

He writes beautiful stories!

You have a beautiful story waiting to be told!

Love your story.

Love your life!

He's a great author."

Mark Kroesch

What negative aspect of your past do you need to surrender to God?

November 2

"The steadfast love of the Lord never ceases;

his mercies never come to an end;

they are new every morning;

great is your faithfulness.

'The Lord is my portion,' says my soul,

'therefore I will hope in him.'"

Lamentations 3:22–24

For what mercies will you give thanks today?

November 3

> "The world outside is getting more brutal every day. We focus on expanding personal energy from the inside to confront it."
>
> *Jim Loehr*

On this election day, after these brutal campaigns, what will be your prayer for peace and healing?

November 4

"Be faithful in small things because it is in them that your strength lies."

Mother Teresa

What small thing in your life needs more attention and focus?

November 5

> "Conformity is the jailer of freedom and the enemy of growth."
> *John F. Kennedy*

Is there an area of your life where you need to think or act outside the box?

November 6

> "Whoever disregards discipline comes to poverty and shame, but whoever heeds correction is honored."
>
> *Proverbs 13:18*

What correction do you need to internalize?

November 7

> "I can't change the direction of the wind, but I can adjust my sails to always reach my destination."
>
> *Jimmy Dean*

What change do you need to make in your life's trajectory?

November 8

"When in doubt physically, dare; when in moral doubt, stop; when in spiritual doubt, pray; and when in personal doubt, be guided by your life with God."

Oswald Chambers

Which of these four doubt categories are you experiencing today? Pray for God's guidance.

November 9

"Every distracted minute is an unrecoverable minute, now frozen in the permanent past. It is right to seek to make the best use of our time in these evil days (Ephesians 5:16).

And yet, we also do not need to be more paralyzed by this than by any other struggle with sin or futility. Our Father wants us to grow in the grace of faith-fueled focus, and will, through Christ, cause our difficult struggles against distraction to work for our good (Romans 8:28). He will, through his Spirit, use them to free us from idolatry and pride and to help us grow in self-control. So, in confident faith we can approach his throne of grace with this prayer:

Whatever it takes, Lord, increase my resolve to pursue only what you call me to do, and deliver me from the fragmenting effect of fruitless distraction."

Jon Bloom, Desiring God blog

How can the Holy Spirit sharpen your focus for the things of Christ? Bring that question to Him in prayer.

November 10

> "When I stand before God at the end of my life, I would hope that I would not have a single bit of talent left and could say, I used everything you gave me."
>
> *Erma Bombeck*

When you stand before God, what account will you give of your life?

November 11

> "The road is long
>
> With many a winding turn
>
> That leads us to who knows where
>
> Who knows where
>
> But I'm strong
>
> Strong enough to carry him
>
> He ain't heavy, he's my brother
>
> ...
>
> And the load
>
> Doesn't weigh me down at all
>
> He ain't heavy he's my brother"
>
> *The Hollies circa 1969*

Veterans often return home with physical or emotional scars. How can you help carry a vet's burden today?

November 12

> "Folks are usually about as happy as they make their minds up to be."
>
> *Abraham Lincoln*

What can you choose to be happy about today?

November 13

"Live simply, love generously, care deeply, speak kindly, leave the rest to God"

Ronald Reagan

Which of these do you want to activate in your life today?

November 14

> "We gain strength, and courage, and confidence by each experience in which we really stop to look fear in the face...we must do that which we think we cannot."
>
> *Eleanor Roosevelt*

What fear in your life needs to brought to Jesus to be smashed by increased Faith?

November 15

"One of the greatest moments in anybody's developing experience is when he no longer tries to hide from himself but determines to get acquainted with himself as he really is."

Norman Vincent Peale

What secret in your life needs to be confessed before Christ?

November 16

"Each person on this planet is here for a purpose...That purpose is to care for other people and to help this world become a better place through service to others."

Gary Sinise

Who is one person who needs a greater amount of care from you?

Here in the Western church, we tend to think of adversity as a bad thing. However, the persecuted church around the world tends to view adversity through a different lens:

"I tell you the truth, unless a kernel of wheat is planted in the soil and dies, it remains alone. But its death will produce many new kernels--a plentiful harvest of new lives." John 12:24

I read the words of a martyred Christian missionary recently. Reflecting on John 12:24, he said shortly before his death in Nigeria at the hands of terrorists: "They tried to bury us. But, what they didn't realize was .... WE WERE SEEDS!"

While it's unlikely that any of us in the United States will be martyred, each of us is going to face oppression from time to time; sometimes intense and severe oppression. As it's happening, I'm going to challenge myself to lean into it, not run from it, and to ask God to use it to "kill" whatever is inside me that's keeping my from a deeper relationship with Christ. As that sin stronghold dies, I'm freed up to be a seed that blossoms and reaches out to encourage others in their walk with our Lord. Even Jesus had to die and be buried, to trigger the Holy Spirit-driven seeds that cascaded down through the centuries and eventually reached each of us.

Fight the good fight, brothers! God's got this.

John 12:24 and Frank Pleticha

Is there a difficult area of your life where you're tempted to run away? Ask God for the strength to stand firm against it. Ask the Spirit to use that adversity to Kill whatever is keeping you from a deeper relationship with Christ Jesus.

November 18

> "Faith does not eliminate questions. But faith knows where to take them."
>
> *Elisabeth Elliot*

What nagging question do you need to take before the Lord in prayer today?

November 19

"We're here to put a dent in the universe. Otherwise why else even be here?"

Steve Jobs

What small step can you take today to begin making a dent in your own universe?

November 20

"If you are honest, truthful, and transparent, people trust you. If people trust you, you have no grounds for fear, suspicion or jealousy."

Dalai Lama

How can you reshape your life to be more transparent?

November 21

> "In ordinary life, we hardly realize that we receive a great deal more than we give, and that it is only with gratitude that life becomes rich."
>
> *Dietrich Bonhoeffer*

What blessings have been showered upon you over the course of your life?

November 22

> "No person was ever honored for what he received. Honor has been the reward for what he gave."
>
> *Calvin Coolidge*

In what ways do you intend to be a better giver?

November 23

> "A joy shared is a joy multiplied, but a pain shared is a pain halved!"
>
> *Vicky Farber*

Do you have a joyful or painful area of your life that needs sharing?

November 24

> "For we are God's masterpiece. He has created us anew in Christ Jesus, so we can do the good things he planned for us long ago." Ephesians 2:10.

It's undeniable that God loves you. He sees you as his masterpiece. Think of that for a moment. The definition of masterpiece is "a work of outstanding artistry, skill, or workmanship." And God is the most talented artist ever. If he created you as a masterpiece, which he did, why don't you see yourself as a masterpiece? See yourself as a masterpiece and go out and make masterpieces. Pursue that purpose. Make everyone better through your example and encouragement. Be kind to all. Love God like he loves you. And see yourself as HE does!

November 25

> "You might not make it to the top, but if you are doing what you love, there is much more happiness there than being rich or famous"
>
> *Unknown*

Are you doing what you love? If not, ask God to help set you on that path.

"When you are thankful, you worship Me acceptably - with reverence and awe. Thanksgiving is not just a holiday celebration once a year. It's an attitude of the heart that produces Joy; it is also a biblical command. You cannot worship Me acceptably with an ungrateful heart. You may go through the motions, but your ingratitude will hold you back.

Whenever you're struggling spiritually or emotionally, pause and check your "thankfulness gauge." If the reading is low, ask Me to help you increase your level of gratefulness. Search for reasons to thank Me; jot them down if you like. Your perspectives will gradually shift from focusing on all that is wrong to rejoicing in things that are right.

No matter what is happening you can be joyful n God your Savior. Because of My finished work on the cross, you have a glorious future that is guaranteed forever! Rejoice in this free gift of salvation - for you, for all who trust Me as a Savior Let your heart overflow with thankfulness, and I will fill you with My Joy."

Jesus Calling by Sarah Young

What joy can you find in your circumstances today? Ask for the Holy Spirit's help in lifting up thanks.

November 27

"Far more often, you must keep showing up, day in and day out, until the hard, unglamorous work adds up and pays off. It's easy to misunderstand what you are seeing when you look at people taking a victory lap or receiving attention or promotion. Their celebration is only the tip of the iceberg. Invisible to your eyes is what's underwater – the hell they went through on the road to success!"

Levi Lusko

What do you need to get done today?

November 28

> "Imagine what our real neighborhoods would be like if each of us offered, as a matter of course, just one kind word to another person."
>
> *Mr. Rogers*

What words or acts of kindness can you offer to someone in your community today?

> "Here's the complete record from Canadian scientist, G.B. Hardy:
>
> The tomb of Buddha – occupied
>
> The tomb of Confucius – occupied
>
> The tomb of Mohammed – occupied
>
> The tomb of Jesus – Empty
>
> Blessed be the God and Father of our Lord Jesus Christ! By great mercy he gave us new birth into a living hope through the resurrection of Jesus Christ from the dead..."
>
> *1 Peter 1:3*

As Advent begins, what can you do to recommit your life such that you're living out your new birth in Christ?

November 30

"Most humans are never fully present in the now, because unconsciously they believe the next moment must be more important than this one. But then you miss your whole life, which is never not now. And that's a revelation for some people. To realize that your life is only ever now."

Eckhart Tolle, writer

How will you strengthen your commitment to be present in the present?

December

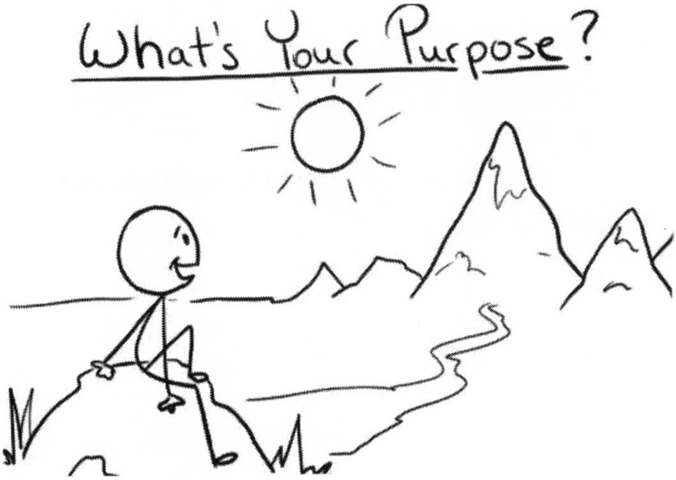
What's Your Purpose?

December 1

> "Everybody's born to be different – that's the one thing that
> makes us the same"
>
> *Meghan Trainor*

Thinking about someone you know -- maybe someone who is a bit different
-- in what ways can you affirm them today?

December 2

> "The person who says something is impossible should not interrupt the person who is doing it."
>
> *George Bernard Shaw*

Are you labelling something as impossible that maybe isn't?

December 3

"When all you have is God, you have all you need."
Dennis Fisher

In your prayers today, how can you surrender to this truth?

December 4

"Life is either a daring adventure or nothing at all"

Helen Keller

What spiritual adventure are you seeking from the Lord?

December 5

> "It is never too late to become what you were always meant to be."
>
> *George Eliot*

Do you think you're too old to live out God's purpose for your life? Ask Him to give you an attitude adjustment.

December 6

One must not focus on the risk of saying, "Yes." The greater risk is missing opportunities by saying, "No."

Bill Gates

Is there an opportunity that you're seeking to avoid?

December 7

> "Good is the enemy of great. Great is the enemy of WORLD CLASS!"
>
> *Jim Collins*

In what part of my life am I settling for "good enough?"

December 8

"Do not merely look out for your own personal interests, but also
for the interests of others."

Philippians 2:4

Who in your life needs your encouragement and advocacy?

December 9

> "The two most important days in your life are the day you were born and the day you find out why."
>
> *Mark Twain*

Are you asking God to reveal your life's purpose?

"Setting a Direction: A Written Manifesto

Beyond evaluating our current life experience and becoming clear as to whether or not our days' efforts are meaningful to us, we must set a new and more proactive course for our lives.

·What will our purpose be from this moment forward?

·What will be our plan of action?

·What steps must be taken?

·What am I really after in life?

·What do I truly want to create and contribute?

·What kind of person do I want to show the world each day?

·What types of persons shall I love and enjoy life with?

·What great cause will keep me going when I feel weak or distracted?

·What shall be my ultimate legacy?

·What steps must I take to begin and sustain these efforts?

·What will I orient my days to accomplishing this week? This month? This year?

Yes, we must write these things down in what will be our own manifesto, our own written declaration of what our lives are to be about."

Brendon Burchard, The Motivation Manifesto: 9 Declarations to Claim Your Personal Power

---

What will be your ultimate legacy? How will people describe you as they reflect on your life during your funeral or memorial service?

December 11

> "Whatever you are doing today, do it with all the confidence of a
> four-year-old in a Batman t-shirt!"
>
> *Liz Mannegren*

What do you need to pray for in order to see your confidence multiplied
today?

December 12

> "Our goal should be to pray such gutsy prayers that God says amen to us!"
>
> *Levi Lusko*

Ask for God's help in praying this surrender prayer: "Holy Spirit, please remove from my life or bring into my life whatever is needed to shape me into the image and likeness of my Lord Jesus Christ." Are you feeling and experiencing the spiritual power today?

December 13

"You, you beautiful, magnificent human, you're just like me.

You will rise up from anything thrown your way.

You will recreate yourself when the vision you had for your career isn't true anymore.

You are not stuck, you are holding yourself back because of the fear that you cannot withstand the pain if you are wounded by the big choices you have to make.

Embrace the chance at scar tissue from trying and falling down.

Believe for just a minute that you are capable of doing more than what you're settling for.

Think I'm not talking to you? I am."

Michaela Alexis

Which of these inspirational thoughts from Michaela do you need to send up as a prayer today? Where do you need the Holy Spirit's inspiration, involvement, and guidance?

December 14

> "Never let the sadness of your past and the fear of your future ruin the happiness of your present!"
>
> *Shannon Mejia*

What past regrets or future fears do you need to surrender in prayer today?

December 15

> "Success is not final, failure is not fatal: it is the courage to continue that counts."
>
> *Winston Churchill*

What words would you lift up in prayer to ask for perseverance?

December 16

> "Attitude is a boomerang: Whatever you throw out there will come back your way."
>
> *John Cena*

Is there a negative attitude that's holding you back or poisoning your drive?

December 17

> "Whoever said revenge is sweet never tasted the yumminess of forget-about-it."
>
> *Karen Salmansohn*

Who do you need to forgive, even if they may not deserve it?

December 18

"Sustain me, my God, according to your promise, and I will live; do not let my hopes be dashed!" -Psalm 119:116

This is a great reminder when things don't go "our" way. Don't give up. Ask for clarity. Buckle down for His will. Chase the Lion!

Psalm 119:116

Pastor Mark Batterson gives a fresh perspective on obstacles we face in life. If you're being tempted to give up, pour out your situation in prayer. What do you need from God to overcome these obstacles?

December 19

> "God does not comfort us to make us comfortable but to make us comforters."
>
> *Billy Graham*

Who needs your comfort during this Advent season?

December 20

> "Just think—you don't need a thing, you've got it all! All God's gifts are right in front of you as you wait expectantly for our Master Jesus to arrive on the scene for the Finale. And not only that, but God himself is right alongside to keep you steady and on track until things are all wrapped up by Jesus. God, who got you started in this spiritual adventure, shares with us the life of his Son and our Master Jesus. He will never give up on you. Never forget that."
>
> *1 Corinthians 1:7-9 MSG*

As the people of this world rush to buy gifts, what prayer for clarity will you lift up to the Lord? What spiritual gift already in your possession needs to make itself known?

December 21

"Having the answers is not essential to living. What is essential is the sense of God's presence during dark seasons of questioning."

Ravi Zacharias

Today, Earth receives the least amount of daylight. In this darkness, what can you take from Scripture concerning God's presence in your life?

December 22

> "Do not go where the path may lead, go instead where there is
> no path and leave a trail."
>
> *Ralph Waldo Emerson*

What new path can you prepare to travel next year?

December 23

"God does not give us everything we want, but He does fulfill His promises, leading us along the best and straightest paths to Himself."

Dietrich Bonhoeffer

As you Journey toward Bethlehem with Christ, what spiritual gift do you seek?

December 24

From Desert Song, by Hillsong United:

"And this is my prayer in the fire

In weakness or trial or pain

There is a faith proved

Of more worth than gold

So refine me Lord through the flames

And I will bring praise

I will bring praise

No weapon forged against me shall remain

I will rejoice

I will declare

God is my victory and He is here

And this is my prayer in the battle

When triumph is still on it's way

I am a conqueror and co-heir with Christ

So firm on His promise I'll stand"

For a massively inspirational experience, you can find the entire song at the link below. When I'm feeling overwhelmed, this song reminds me of where I stand in Christ.

https://www.youtube.com/watch?v=HUISd7LSxAQ *Hillsong United*

Two bookends. Today, we celebrate the birth of the Author of our Salvation. Jesus surrendered His Heavenly Throne and chose to walk among us. About 33 years later, He would choose in the supreme act of Love to surrender His life for us on the Cross. What aspect of your life do you need to surrender for Crucifixion? Present this surrendered and cleansed part of your life as your birthday gift to baby Jesus.

I am the word that became flesh. I have always been, and I will always be. In the beginning was the Word, and the Word was with God, and the Word was God. As you think about Me as a baby, born in Bethlehem, do not lose sight of My divinity. This baby who grew up and became a Man-Savior is also God Almighty! It could not have been otherwise. My sacrificial life and death would have been insufficient if I were not God. So rejoice that the Word, who entered the world as a helpless infant, is the same One who brought the world into existence.

Though I was rich, for your sake I became poor, so that you might become rich. No Christmas present could ever compare with the treasure you have in Me! I remove your sins as far as the east is from the west -- freeing you from all condemnation. I gift you with unimaginably glorious Life that will never end! The best response to this astonishing Gift is to embrace it joyfully and gratefully.

Sarah Young, Jesus Always

Today, Christmas Day, as you open your gifts, will you stop to remember and give thanks to the most glorious, everlasting gift you could possibly receive? Eternal life in the Kingdom of Heaven? Praise the Lord.

December 26

| "It is Finished" |
| Jesus in John 19:30 |

Yesterday, we celebrated our Lord's arrival on Earth. But in this short passage from the Gospel of John, we see today some of His last words on the Cross. What will be your prayer of thanks for this gift of Salvation?

December 27

A reminder of two things:

1. Each of us is still a work in process.

2. But, despite our progress or lack of progress on a given day, our Lord IS going to finish that work.

Be encouraged, brothers!

"And I am certain that God, who began the good work within you, will continue his work until it is finally finished on the day when Christ Jesus returns."

Philippians 1:6

What is one area of your life where you're beating yourself up from your lack of progress? Embrace this promise from God's Word that the Holy Spirit will never give up on you.

December 28

"But one thing I do: forgetting what lies behind and straining forward to what lies ahead, I press on toward the goal for the prize of the upward call of God in Christ Jesus"

Philippians 3:13–14

What help do you need from the Holy Spirit to press on?

December 29

> "Chase the Lion is not just a book - it's a call to action. Jesus didn't die just to keep you safe. He died to make you dangerous. Carpe Diem!"
>
> *Mark Batterson, Chase the Lion*

What would be the words you'd use in a "make me dangerous" prayer?

December 30

> "I heard a loud voice speaking from the throne: "Now God's home is with human beings! He will live with them, and they shall be his people. God himself will be with them, and he will be their God. He will wipe away all tears from their eyes. There will be no more death, no more grief or crying or pain. The old things have disappeared."
>
> *Revelation 21:3-4*

The old things of this year are rapidly passing away. What does your heart and soul need from Jesus to live in a joyful state in the new year?